Ninety-Five

Bosey

Ninety-Five

Meeting America's Farmed Animals
in Stories and Photographs

EDITED BY NO VOICE UNHEARD

ISBN: 978-0-9728387-5-7
Library of Congress Control Number: 2009935190
First Edition 2010

Design and production by Prism Photographics, Inc., Carson City, NV

Printed in Singapore

Text © No Voice Unheard except the following:

Amelia: Gentle Companion
Jeremy & Lenny: The Destiny of a Toddler
Sanctuary: A Day in Their Lives
 © Davida Gypsy Breier

Charley: At Work
 © Eric Davis, DVM

Olivia: Teach Your Children
Ralphie - Andy - Elvis: Gentle Giants
 © Bob Esposito

Dutch: A Duck's Best Friend
Linda & Tricia: BBFF
Lucky Lady: Lessons Learned
 © Farm Sanctuary Inc.

Introduction: Gilly's Story
 © Marilee Geyer

Farrah & Damien: The Gift of Their Presence
Justice: … For They Shall Be Comforted
 © Diane Leigh

Goosifer: The Goose Formerly Known as Lucifer
Libby & Louie: A Love Story
Lucas: Pig Love
Marcie: Portrait of a Beautiful Soul
Melvin: Sun Day
 © Joanna Lucas

Sophie: Finding Our Way Together
 © Jean Rhode

Ariala & Rhoslyn: Beating the Odds
 © Kit Salisbury

Madeline: Brave Bird
 © Windi Wojdak

All photographs are copyrighted to the credited photographer.

Photographs credited to Natalie Bowman, Susie Coston and Erin Howard are the copyright of Farm Sanctuary Inc.

Thomas Berry quote from *A Language Older Than Words,* by Derrick Jensen

In honor and in memory of all animals, everywhere.

PO Box 4171
Santa Cruz, CA 95063
(831) 440-9574
info@novoiceunheard.org
www.NoVoiceUnheard.org

Contents

Introduction

GILLY'S STORY

She's two and a half years old and has all the energy you'd expect of a toddler. She has two speeds: run and stop. All things new pique her curiosity and she's inquisitive beyond reason. Her favorite activities are eating, lounging in the sun, bathing in dust, and more eating – she has a special affinity for watermelon, pasta and corn. She experiences a wide variety of emotions, but joy and contentment are the two she expresses most often. During the day she often sits on my lap or rests quietly at my feet while I work at the computer. At night she sleeps warm and secure on a bed of straw and shavings with her three other companions.

Gilly is a white Leghorn hen. Her life now is a world apart from the world into which she was born.

⇒◆⇐

When animal advocates received word that a commercial egg facility in northern California was closing down and that the land owner was going to allow animal groups to take as many hens as they could find homes for, they jumped into action. Volunteers from all over the area networked, made phone calls, and sent emails, arranging crates and transportation and care for as many birds as they possibly could.

When they got to the "farm," prepared to rescue over 500 chickens, they were astonished to find one hundred and sixty thousand. *One hundred and sixty thousand.*

⇒◆⇐

It was a beautiful, blue sky morning when the volunteers gathered. The egg factory consisted of one large, windowless building, the size of many football fields. As I walked to the door to go inside, I wondered what I would find. This particular facility held Leghorns, the most commonly-used breed in the egg industry. I'd seen pictures of these types of factory farms, but actually experiencing it firsthand was completely different. It's hard to adequately describe the horror of the facility: the right words are difficult to find.

Inside, the warm and humid air was thick with dust, feathers and grime. The smell in the closed building was overwhelming: a putrid combination of feces, ammonia, dead birds and stale eggs. The sound was deafening: 160,000 birds squawked and screeched, and conveyor belts bringing food and taking away eggs roared. Row after row of metal cages, extending as far into the filth as I could see were stacked three high. Each cage was stuffed with seven to eight hens, their beaks cut off to prevent them from pecking each other and the birds on the bottom were brown and dirty — you'd never know their natural color was white. These hens were living lives of unimaginable misery and suffering.

As I approached the cages, I didn't know which hens to take. How do you choose when surrounded by so many suffering animals? In the end I randomly chose a bank of cages and, as gently as I could, lifted hens out of cages and into waiting crates where they would be taken to a series of foster and permanent homes.

In the end, various animal organizations were able to rescue over 1,000 hens, but that meant that the rest would go to slaughter, and I cried as I watched the slaughter truck, packed with birds, drive away to its awful destination. And despite the fact that the hens rescued that day would now live in comfort, I could not forget the more than 159,000 that would soon die and the more than 300 million commercial egg-laying hens living in the United States under these deplorable conditions, with few laws to protect them. They live short, wretched lives: the poultry industry considers them "spent" within two years, after which they endure a terrifying trip to a slaughter plant where they have an even more terrifying and painful death.

⟞⟶◆⟵⟝

I became guardian of 57 of the rescued hens and took them to a barn at a local animal shelter, where I would care for them until they were ready to move to permanent homes. As I unloaded the crates from my truck, I was shocked to find them filled with eggs. Throughout the rescue and the long trip to the shelter, their bodies were still laying eggs, testament to the genetic manipulation inflicted on them by humans, which programs them to lay eggs rapidly, no matter what the circumstances.

After unlatching the crate doors, I stood close by, waiting for the hens to come out into the stall I had prepared. They wouldn't come out. I slowly removed the tops of the crates so that they could see where they were. Still they stood, afraid even to move their heads and look around. I gently lifted them out, setting them on the thick, soft bed of shavings laid out for them. Still they stood in place, not moving. Were they too scared? Stunned? In shock? Uncomfortable with the open space after being so confined? Was the quietness of the barn strange to them? Still they stood, some, heartbreakingly, laying more eggs.

I didn't dare open the stall door to the outside area; I thought they'd be completely overwhelmed. Perches were set up for them to use, but they didn't. Instead, I put some extra large crates in the stall for them to hide in, and eventually they did.

The next morning, they ventured out of the crates and explored their new surroundings. I opened the door to the corral, a grassy and dirt area in full sunlight. Some stood at the edge of the door and looked out. After an hour, a few brave birds stepped outside, tentatively. Over a period of days, most of the hens made their way outside. Some spent a lot of time outside, some only rarely; already, each was developing her own personal preferences.

Each day when I came to care for them, I spoke softly and moved slowly. After a few days, they stopped running to the other side of the stall when I came in. I would greet them, "Hey girls, hello you pretty girls" and after awhile, some chattered in response.

I brought them fresh watermelon. Only the braver birds approached this new and strange item. They stared at it, not knowing what to do. Finally, one pecked at it, unleashing a melon free-for-all. Watermelon became one of their favorite treats and their white feathers were often stained pink from excess juice running from their mouths down to their chests.

I left bales of pine shavings, letting them take the bales apart. They kicked the shavings to loosen them, and carved caves into the bales. They seemed to enjoy building their own nests to lay their eggs. Initially, they continued to lay eggs at a frantic pace, then the pace slowed down. They began to use the perches.

When I cleaned crates, water flowed, creating mud puddles which proved an irresistible attraction. They marched in, stomped their feet, dug in the mud. Clearly, they were enjoying themselves.

I loved sitting quietly in the stall, not only to help them get used to people, but to just be present with them and communicate with my voice and hands and eyes: you're safe now. I began to recognize who was who. I saw physical differences, and differences in personalities. Some of the hens were more curious than others. Some were shy, and some were very bold. Some were energetic. Some had beaks that were more mutilated than others, and had more difficulty eating. Some had legs that were more yellow than others. Each was her own individual, yet they all had a resiliency that was humbling to witness. And although every small step they took toward life was challenging, they took those steps, they healed… they wanted to live.

Two weeks after rescue, the change in the hens was enormous.

Having never been outside, having never walked on the ground, they now scratched the earth looking for insects, reveled in the pleasure of dust baths, and napped in the warm sun. Their beautiful white feathers slowly began to grow back and their combs and wattles became healthy and pink. They enthusiastically accepted treats of fresh greens, blueberries, and tomatoes. They began to trust and became more confident each day. They experienced, for the first time, peace and comfort.

Eventually they ran to me when I came in. Gilly was one of the first to run up to me. And when I left the stall doors open, she followed me out. I started leaving the doors open while doing my chores, so that she could follow me around the barn. When the hens were ready to be adopted out to permanent homes, Gilly came home with me.

I already shared my backyard with three hens, and wanted to introduce Gilly gradually to the already-established group, but she would have none of that. She squawked at the gate of the enclosure I put her in. When I let her out, she ran straight to the other hens and settled in, as if to say "Here I am." Gilly was exuberant to the extreme, running and crashing into the others, who accepted her with patience and grace.

Gilly investigated every square inch of her new quarter acre yard, and found the areas with the most plentiful bugs and tender grass (unfortunately, both in my garden beds!). She chattered constantly, schooling me in chicken language: the big squawking bwak-bwak-bwak that accompanies egg laying; the kkkk-ka-kkkk muttering of happily patrolling the back yard; the friendly bu-buuu-bu hello that greeted me each morning.

Like everyone who loves animals and shares a home with them, I know what my dog wants by the look in his eyes, or how my cat feels from her body language. When I adopted my first two chickens from a local rescue group, I had little experience living with birds, much less chickens. Of course, many people have birds as companions: parakeets, cockatoos and parrots. But our culture has trained us to think of "poultry," of farmed animals, as entirely different. We learn from an early age that some animals are "pets;" others are "food." We are purposely kept from knowing the truth about the nature of these animals and the conditions in which they live and die. The animal agriculture industry likes it that way because if you knew the truth, if you made a connection, you'd know there's no reason at all to assume that a chicken could be any less endearing than a parakeet, a retriever or a tabby cat. Drawing that distinction in language certainly helps us in distinguishing a potential pet from a potential dinner, however, and maybe that's what it all boils down to.

But a linguistic distinction is just a theoretical construct, and theory meant nothing to Gilly. She had as much depth and personality and life as any of my canine and feline companions. Which makes it all the more heartbreaking to think of them – hundreds of millions of them a year – living the way Gilly did. The enormity of the suffering is unimaginable.

———❖———

The photograph of Gilly at the beginning of this story is the best one I have. I didn't take many pictures of her; I always thought there was plenty of time to do that. But I was wrong. The human beings who bred her, who genetically manipulated her to produce lots of eggs, and to produce and produce and produce, didn't intend her to live very long.

The body that was designed to turn out an unnatural amount of eggs at an unnatural rate finally failed her, and when she could no longer keep up with the physical demands of such production, she fell ill, and then, just like that – in a breath, in a heartbeat – she was gone. She died in my hands.

Gilly shared her joyful spirit and her life with me. I will always be grateful for the glorious spark of life in her eyes, the quiet peaceful moments we shared and all the times I looked out my kitchen window to see her in the backyard. Happy. Safe.

Now I share Gilly's life with you. I share it in honor of Glynda, Gilda and Wilhelmia who were rescued along with Gilly from the egg factory that day. And I share it in memory of the one hundred and fifty-nine thousand hens who were left behind.

— *Marilee Geyer*

Glynda

Gilda

Wilhelmina

A Note from the Editors

In a very real way, Gilly was the inspiration for this book. We were all sitting in Marilee's yard, watching Gilly dart joyfully back and forth across the grass, and watching the other chickens scratch and strut and dig. We laughed at how they all wanted to dig right where Marilee had decided to plant some cilantro – the digging was obviously fun but the cilantro had to be moved to another part of the garden. Each chicken in the little flock was being thoroughly herself – Tulip, deliberate and intense in her activity; Edwina, clearly the one in charge, checking out what everyone else was doing; Emelina, the diva, first one out of the hen house, first one at everything; and Minnie, the quiet and dignified, 14-year-old "old soul." It was a peaceful, picture-perfect afternoon, quiet, the chickens' little cluckings and cooings providing background music, everyone – people and chickens – happy and content.

Diane commented, "I wish everyone could see these chickens, on a day like this – how happy they are, what they love, how much personality each one has – people would be amazed."

Thus the idea for *Ninety-Five* was born.

———⟫•⟪———

Ninety-five is an often-cited figure for the number of animals saved yearly by one person's vegan diet. Picture that: ninety-five animals, each year. Astounding. The number is an estimate, of course, but roughly accurate. It includes not just animals we eat, but also animals who are farmed for something other than their meat – their eggs, or their milk. Also, a significant portion of that number is made up of aquatic animals.

[A note about terminology is appropriate here: it's really not accurate to call them "farm" animals. Really, they're "farmed" animals – farming is something that's done *to* them. Many people have changed their language to use this term when referring to them.]

———⟫•⟪———

At first we thought we knew what kind of book we wanted to write: a comprehensive examination of modern animal agriculture practices. We wanted to create an informative and educational book describing the conditions that farmed animals live, and die, in. We wanted to tell you what ten billion Gillys a year go through in this country's unimaginably cruel factory farming systems, and that even non-factory type farms have their own inherent cruelties.

Rudy

But getting to know Gilly changed that. This book doesn't focus on the details of modern agriculture and factory farming; we don't talk about greenhouse gases and pollution and the other environmental impacts of raising animals for food, or how many hungry people could be fed by the food we feed to farmed animals. Excellent books have already been published that cover all these critically important topics and we've listed some of our favorites in the back of this book should you wish to learn more.

No, we decided what we really want to do is to just have you meet the animals, and show you what they're like when they're allowed to be who they are. We want to introduce you to these amazing and charming creatures, and their remarkable personalities, emotions, relationships, desires and depth. We want to invite you into Marilee's backyard, so to speak, to meet some of the ninety-five animals who are spared, in one year, by one person's vegan diet.

So, we visited farmed animal sanctuaries across the country, meeting dozens of animals who were rescued from a variety of farming-related situations and brought to these places of safety. These animals now live in peace, and will be cared for by devoted staff and volunteers for the rest of their lives. Some of the sanctuaries are large, well-developed non-profit organizations; others are simply people who decided they could offer a home to a formerly-farmed animal or two. All of our visits, and all of the people and animals, were completely inspiring.

It is important to note here that, as far as we know, there are no sanctuaries or rescue organizations focusing on farmed fish or other aquatic animals, so regrettably, they are not included in the stories in this book. Their lives should not be forgotten or dismissed, however, and so we include a special section about them later.

Quite a number of the people we met, who care for and about farmed animals are moved to honor these animals in writing and photography. This book is a collection of their work. Their writings include a variety of voices, from informal to elegant, but all share a passionate desire to tell you how much more there is to these animals than most of us realize. Their photos are equally passionate, fueled by the love and respect each photographer holds for their subject. It's a powerful package, and we are proud to share it with you.

Peapod

We invite you to meet these animals. Some of these stories will make you chuckle, some will move you, some may bring tears to your eyes, and some will just plain give you something to think about. We know that you will enjoy the stunning photos, too, and when you look into the eyes of these animals, note the spark of life in those eyes. It is the same treasured spark we see in our dogs' and cats' eyes, the same beloved spark we see in the eyes of our friends and family. These animals could be family, too … and the first step is meeting them.

— *Marilee Geyer, Diane Leigh and Windi Wojdak*

Francine

Rhubarb

Francine & Iris

Benjamin

Violet

Julia, Zenobia & Jolene

Elinor

Goldie

Kathleen

Madeline

BRAVE BIRD

I don't know the details of Madeline's life before she came to live with me. I can only speculate on where she was born or how she came to be in the situation in which she was found. I do know that she was rescued by an animal control officer responding to a complaint that a woman was keeping forty chickens in a coop only large enough for ten. They had no food or water and several were ill or injured. When confronted by the officer, the woman relinquished custody of the sick and wounded birds, as well as most of the others. The ailing hens were immediately taken by the officer to a veterinarian for treatment. That's where I met Madeline. Responding to a call for foster homes, I picked Madeline up at the hospital just a few days after her rescue to care for her until her injuries had healed and she could be adopted into a permanent home.

The day Madeline came home with me, broken and near death, I thought certainly she would never make it. A painful joint infection had left her unable to walk or even stand. Incapable of reaching food, she had lost weight and had been pecked by some of the other birds, opening a large laceration on her head that had become infected. Her injuries and lack of nutrition had left her so weak she was unable to lift her head for more than a few moments. Her prognosis was guarded, and almost immediately I began to second guess my decision to try to save her. Would treatment just prolong her suffering?

I brought her inside my home, made her a comfortable nest in a large dog crate and set about caring for this brave bird. Even though she was quite ill, Madeline radiated a spark, a will, an intensity that let me know she wanted to live. Eventually, after many days of treating her injuries, waiting and hoping, and wondering whether the subtle improvements I thought I was seeing were real or just wishful thinking, Madeline lifted herself on to her weakened legs. For just a moment she stood before she buckled again to the floor. It wasn't much, but it was enough to tell me that I had made the right decision.

Gradually, over several weeks, Madeline pushed herself through the pain and weakness until she was standing and walking. Often she would settle in beside me as I worked. Resting her head on my leg while I scratched the delicate skin under her wings, she would close her eyes in complete contentment. Her interest in me was a bit of a surprise: her limited experience with humans had been one of indifference and cruelty, and she had no reason to trust me, but she did, and I was thrilled by her desire to be near me.

As she regained her strength, she strutted about as though she owned the world. She met the cats and dogs who live with me and began exploring the world outside. She never seemed to doubt her own power, but acted as if she knew exactly who she was, moving through her day with enviable confidence in herself and her abilities.

As much as I loved sharing my home with her, eventually I had to admit that Madeline was healthy enough to go to a new, permanent home. She needed a safe outside space in which to peck and preen, and she needed the company of other chickens. She was adopted by a friend who had a small flock of chickens living freely in a large backyard.

Madeline moved right in and in the company of other hens, her personality began to shine. In the beginning, she was content to eat out of her food dish and then sit in the shade for a good part of the day, but her flock-mates soon showed her all the best places to scratch for bugs and taught her how delicious green grass is to graze on.

Contrasted against the greenery and seasonal wildflowers of her backyard, she was stunningly beautiful: lustrous white feathers, a vivid red comb and wattles on a bright red face, a yellow beak and deep yellow legs and toes. And she was big. Really big. Almost three times the weight of a typical hen. Madeline was a Cornish mix; a breed the poultry industry calls a "broiler." She was designed to gain a lot of weight very quickly and go to slaughter at only 49 days old, still a baby. Because of this unnatural breeding, "broilers" often have joint and ligament problems and suffer from congestive heart failure. Despite her size, Madeline was surprisingly agile and could charge down the backyard hill as fast as any of the other hens if there was a treat to be had.

Madeline had an equally large and endearing personality. She radiated a reassuring energy that comforted the whole group. Madeline was exceedingly brave. Whoever decided that the word "chicken" was an accurate euphemism for cowardly definitely got it wrong. Although running from danger is often the most prudent form of self-defense for chickens, in fact, they can be quite assertive, especially if they're protecting their babies. Madeline took on the role of flock defender and proved to be very courageous. When the appropriately-named chicken hawks flew over the yard, one of the other hens would call out a warning squawk and everyone would run for the nearest cover. Many times that cover was Madeline. While the other girls huddled around her, she would rise on her legs, stretch her neck out toward the sky and stand defiant. When unknown cats found their way into the hens' territory, she would confront them and peck them away if necessary. She was fearless when it came to defending her flock-mates.

Madeline lived happily in the yard with her hen friends for several carefree months before her genetics caught up with her. One morning she lumbered out of her henhouse and promptly sat down, unable to rise again. The bright red of her comb and wattles turned at first a light blue, and then a deeper purple. Madeline's heart was not pumping well enough to circulate oxygen-rich blood through her body. She was rushed to a veterinarian but nothing could be done to relieve her discomfort or heal her over-burdened heart. She lay in the oxygenated cage panting, slowly dying. When the gut-wrenching decision was made to help her pass from this world, she died with dignity and grace. She was only seven months old.

I learned much from Madeline. I learned that hope is never wasted. Hope is what brought her home from the veterinary hospital that first day, and hope is what helped fuel her recovery. I was also reminded of something I already knew but the world often forgets: animals, even the most dis-regarded animals, have rich and varied emotional lives.

They form deep friendships and strong connections with all kinds of beings, not just their own kind. They have their own lives to lead, and they enjoy those lives tremendously. And they have value, simply because they are.

—*Windi Wojdak*

Libby & Louie

A Love Story

It took extraordinary events – a shattering blow, like the loss of her right foot to the wire floor of the "cage-free" egg farm where she was rescued from, or a rapturous release, like her arrival at the sanctuary, or a seismic shift like Louie's absence – to shake, charm, or punish a sound out of Libby. It's not that her voice was frozen in fear, like so many of her fellow refugees. It's not that she was shy, feeble, injured, or ill. She was quiet. And, unlike so many of her kin, she did not enjoy, or need to, commit her inner experiences to the stream of constant humming that often fills chicken communities with the music of their thoughts. Libby's thoughts were silent. Silence was her nature, her disposition, her remedy, her talent, her power, her gift, and her pleasure. She looked at the world in soundless wonder – her thoughts, streaming and darting, swelling and swarming in the dark pools of her eyes – and filled it with the hush of her mind.

In the blush of her first weeks at the sanctuary, when everything astonished her – the open sky, the endless fields, the scent of rain, the feel of straw underfoot – we thought we heard her voice a few times: small, joyful cries coming out of nowhere, seemingly formed out of thin air, the musical friction of invisible particles, not the product of straining, vibrating, trembling vocal cords, but a sound of pure joy coming from the heart of life itself. But, after she paired up with Louie and became his sole partner, Libby turned so completely quiet, that we began to wonder if the voice we had heard in the beginning was truly hers.

Louie's delight in the sound and functioning of his own magnificent voice, his pleasure in putting sound faces on everything – their finds and failures, their contentments and complaints, their yearnings and fears, their joys and hopes, the major, minor or minute events of their daily lives together – gave Libby the improbable ability of being heard without making a sound. For the first time in her life, she could enjoy the bliss of silence and the full power of voice at the same time. Her thoughts, her needs, her feelings, her pleasures and displeasures, were all there – perfectly voiced, perfectly formed, perfectly delivered in Louie's utterings – each experience, captured in the jewel of a flawlessly pitched note. And in these notes, you could hear the developing musical portrait of Libby's inner happenings.

There was the sighed coo for Libby's request to slide under his wing, the raspy hiss for her alarm at OJ, the "killer" cat's approach, the purred hum for her pleasure in dustbathing, the bubbling trill for her enjoyment in eating pumpkin seeds straight out of the pumpkin's cool core on a summer day, the grinding creak for her tiredness, the rusty grumble for her achy joints.

There was the growing vocabulary of songs used to voice their shared moments of delight – the lucky find of the treasure trove hidden in a compost pile, discovered by Libby and dug out with Louie's help to reveal a feast of riches to taste, eat, explore, investigate or play with; or the gift of walking side by side into the morning sun and greeting a new day together; or the adventure of sneaking into the pig barn and chasing the flies that landed on the backs of the slumbering giants.

Occasionally, there were the sound bursts for their shared moments of displeasure, hurt, sadness, fear, or downright panic, such as the time when Libby got accidentally locked in a barn that was being cleaned and Louie, distressed at the sudden separation, paced frantically up and down the narrow path on the other side of the closed door, crowing his alarm, crying his pleas, clucking his commands, flapping his wings, showering us with a spray of fervid whistles, following us around, then running back to the barn door, clacking at it, knocking on it, then running back to us, whirring his wings, stomping his feet, tapping the ground with his beak, staring intently, and generally communicating Libby's predicament in every "language" available to him: sound, movement, gaze, color, and certainly scent too.

But, for all of their panache, Louie's most spectacular acts of voice were not his magnificently crafted and projected vocal announcements but his quiet acts of allegiance, his tacit acts of devotion, his daily acts of restraint. The things he did not do.

There was the silent song of giving up his treasured roost in the rafters, his nest in the sky where he had bunked every night of his years before Libby, the space where he felt safest surrendering to sleep, strongest entering the night. Happiest. The spot closest to the clouds. His personal Olympus. But, in her lameness, Libby couldn't join him there. She managed to climb next to him a few times but, with only one foot to grip the perch, she kept losing her balance and fell to the ground and, after a while, she stopped trying and just stayed there, grounded, anchored to the earth. So Louie quietly descended

from his blue yonder and settled next to her in her terrestrial roost – a long, narrow tent created by a leaning plywood board – and he slept near the entrance, exposing himself to the intrusions of curious goats, wandering cats and restless geese, the better to protect Libby from them.

There was the soundless song of limiting the sport of his summer days to fewer and fewer hours when the stiffness in Libby's stump increased with age, and the effort of following Louie in the fields, hobbling and wobbling behind him, turned from tiring to exhausting in fewer and fewer steps, and she started to retire to their nest earlier and earlier in the day. At first, she was able to make it till 6 in the evening, but then 6 became 5, and 5 became 4, and then it was barely 3 in the glorious middle of a summer day when she felt too weary to go on. The day was still in its full splendor, there was still so much more of its gift to explore and experience, and there was still so much energy and curiosity left in Louie to explore with, but Libby was tired, and she had to go to her tent under the plywood plank, and rest her aching joints. And Louie followed. With Libby gone from the dazzling heart of the summer day, the night came early for both of them.

Then there was the tacit song of forfeiting his foraging expeditions and his place in the larger sanctuary community only to be with her. When Libby's advancing age, added to the constant burden of her lameness, forced her to not only shorten her travels with Louie, but end them altogether, and when her increased frailness forced her to seek a more controlled environment than their plywood tent in the barn, she retired to the small, quiet refuge of the House. And Louie followed her there, too, even though he still enjoyed the wide open spaces, the wilder outdoors, the hustle and bustle of bunking in the barn. But Libby needed the extra comfort of the smaller, warmer, more predictable space inside the house and, even though Louie did not, he followed her anyway. And, when she started to spend more and more time indoors, curtailing her already brief outings, Louie did too.

And there they were. Just the two of them in the world. A monogamous couple in a species where monogamy is the exception. Determined to stay together even though their union created more problems than it solved, increased their burdens more than it eased them, and thwarted their instincts more than it fulfilled them.

It would have been easier and more "natural" for Louie to be in charge of a group of hens, like all the other roosters, but he ignored everyone except Libby. He paid no attention to the fluffy grey hen, the fiery blonde hen, the dreamy red hen, the sweet black hen dawdling in her downy pantaloons, or any of the 100 snow-white hens who, to our dim perceptions, looked exactly like Libby. Louie, the most resplendently bedecked and befeathered rooster of the sanctuary, remained devoted only to Libby — scrawny body, scraggly feathers, missing foot, hobbled gait and all. It's true that, with our dull senses, we couldn't grasp a fraction of what he saw in her because we can't see, smell, hear, touch, taste, sense a scintilla of the sights, scents, sounds, textures, and tastes he does. But, even if we could see Libby in all her glory, it would still be clear that it wasn't her physical attributes that enraptured Louie. If he sought her as his one and only companion, if he protected that union from all intrusions, it wasn't because of her physique but because of her presence.

It would have been easier for Libby too — so vulnerable in her stunted, lame body — to join an existing chicken family and enjoy the added comfort, cover and protection of a larger group, but she never did. She stayed with Louie, and followed him on his daily treks in the open fields, limping and gimping behind him, exhausting herself only to be near him.

What bonded them was not about practical necessities or instinctual urges — if anything, it thwarted both. Their union was about something else, a rich inner abundance that seemed to flourish in each other's presence, and that Libby nurtured in her silence and that Louie voiced, sang out loud, celebrated, noted, catalogued, documented, expressed, praised every day of their 1,800 days together.

Except today. Today, it was Libby who "spoke" for both of them. And, this time, there was no doubt whose voice it was, or what it was saying, because it not only sounded off, it split open the sky, punctured the clouds, issued forth with such gripping force and immediacy that it stopped you dead in your tracks. It was a sound of such pure sorrow and longing, hanging there all alone, in stark and immaculate solitude, high above the din of sanctuary life, like the heart-piercing cry of an albatross. She had started to cluck barely audibly at dawn, when Louie failed to get up and lingered listlessly in their nest. She continued her plaintive murmur into the afternoon, when Louie became too weak to hold his head up and collapsed in a heap of limp feathers. And then, when we scooped him up and quarantined him into a separate room for treatment, her soft lament turned to wrenching wail.

The next morning, she was still sounding out her plea, her love, her desperation as she feverishly searched every open room in the house, then wandered out into the small front yard, then the larger back yard, and the small barns behind it. Soon, she left the house and the fenced yard and took her search to the open fields, cooing, calling, crying like a strange sky creature, using her voice as a beacon, it seemed, a sound trail for Louie to follow back to safety, and roaming farther than she had in months, stumbling and staggering on a foot and a stump, the light in her being dimming with every solitary minute, her eyes widened as if struggling to see in dark, her feathers, frayed at the edges, as though singed by the flames of an invisible fire, their sooted ends sticking out like thorns straight from the wound of her soul, her whole being looking tattered and disoriented, as if lost in a suddenly foreign world.

And, for three excruciating days, we didn't dare hope she'd ever find him alive again. Louie was very weak, hanging to life by a thread that seemed thinner and thinner with each passing hour. He didn't respond to the treatment we were advised to give him and, after three days of failed attempts, we were beginning to accept that there was nothing more we could do except to keep him comfortable, hydrated and quiet until the end.

But we underestimated both his strength and her determination. Libby did find her soul mate again. We don't know how she managed to get into the locked rehab room, but she did. We were planning to reunite them later that day – going against the veterinarian's advice, as we sometimes do out of mercy for the animals – because it had become clear to us that Louie's ailment was not contagious, it was "just" a bad fit of old age. But Libby beat us to it. She found her way into his room, only she knows how, and Louie found his way back to life too, seemingly at the same moment. There he was, looking up for the first time in days, life flaring in his eyes again, and there she was, huddled next to him, quietly sharing his hospital crate. And there they still are, Louie, slowly recovering, and Libby, blissfully silent again. She hasn't moved since. She won't leave his side now that she's found him again, she refuses to even look away from him, as if he might disappear in one blink of her eye, as if the force of her gaze alone can keep him anchored in life.

She beholds him with her deep, black eyes, thoughts streaming and darting, swelling and swarming in their dark pools, and she envelops him in her symphonic silence, which – you hear it now! – is not really a silence, but a space in which Louie's voice may shine, a protected space where his voice may grow stronger, vaster, freer – not because it can boom against her muteness, but because it can speak for someone other than himself and, in so doing, it may grow from an instrument of self expression to an instrument of grace. Not the abstract concept of grace that we like to discuss and dissect, but the daily practice and experience of it.

They are both quiet now – Louie, exhausted from his ailment, regaining his strength, Libby, exhausted from her dark journey, gazing steadily at him. Both, brimming, basking in the rich silence that is so alive with voice and flowing conversation, that it glows between them like a strange treasure. And it shines.

– *Joanna Lucas*

Krusty

Johnny

Rootie

Fiona

Andy, Tim & Joan Jett

Patsy

Maggie & Aurora

Rosie & Ronnie

Lucas

Pig Love

Pigs may "speak" the same emotional language as all other sentients – same desires, same hopes, same loves – but they look like us doing it – wrinkled noses, smiling lips, round cheeks, bare bellies and all – and the feeling of resemblance is probably mutual. They smile, spy, inquire, scold with their eyes, they gape in wonder, they cheat with calculated coolness, they slump in defeat, they shrug in confusion, they laugh out loud with open-mouthed enthusiasm, they play pranks, they play video games, they take showers, they get drunk given half a chance, they wallow in the mud in the best sense of the word: literally, copiously, with innocent and earthy abandon, they raise families together, swap nanny duties, sing to their babies while nursing. They sleep prodigally, and dream vividly, and they do it together, as a form of communion, communication and community building. They have favorite friends and favorite foes. They hold grudges, they forgive. They make eye contact with the clear understanding that eyes are where questions are asked, and answered. They fall in love like we do – to the exclusion of everyone else, madly, passionately, desperately in love.

Lucas, for instance, is in love with Petunia. There are eight other sows in his adoptive sounder. He eats with them, hangs out with them, cribs with them. They're friends, they do what friends do – play, banter, argue, bicker, make up, learn from each other, tease each other, forgive each other, keep each other warm, share the pleasures and perils of the soul together. Ernestine, Agnes, Bessie, Elsie, Iris, Charlotte, Sienna, and Sunshine. None of them compares to Petunia.

Petunia is wild, independent, self-sufficient. She walks alone, sleeps alone, eats alone, ignores the pig sounder, ignores visitors, ignores Lucas. She is a maverick, a loner, happiest in her own company.

To most sanctuary residents, she is someone to avoid. To Lucas, she is someone to adore – well worth leaving his hard earned place in his adoptive sounder for, well worth leaving his other projects and explorations, worth forsaking food and water for. She stops him dead in his tracks. She is compelling, arresting, electrifying. With her, in her presence, he seems to find that mysterious something he craves, that something which is worth pursuing even at the risk of unleashing Petunia's wrath.

Lucas is a risk taker. An explorer. Driven by pigly "what ifs?," "what elses?," "whys?," "hows?" A sui(dae) generis adventurer. Happiest in unknown territory, happiest if there's resistance, a force to push against, life that doesn't yield, but pushes back, like a sort of dynamic stability. A swinely swashbuckler. Driven by the need to influence the world around him rather than conform to its offerings (and his constant questioning and challenging of the world inevitably changes it). What, to others, is only a towel drying on a fence, to him is a potential link, a possible portal into something much bigger. What, to others, is the wild and furious pig known as Petunia, to him is wild, dangerous, virgin territory – a place no one else is willing to go, and the only destination that interests him – something irresistible.

Most of the time, his hunch that there is more to things than meets the eye is confirmed. For instance, pulling on that towel was far more than a tug on a soggy piece of terry cloth drying on a fence. It ended up being a cataclysm. It resulted in a series of events that brought down the entire fence, released a small flock of quarantined chickens into the pond yard, almost caused them to drown, and created a commotion of a magnitude that no one looking at that small napkin would have imagined. Similarly, jumping off the truck that was taking him and his family to their final fattening place was far more than a leap. It resulted in a series of events that saved his life, secured his future, and opened a new world. Literally.

He is a discoverer. Consumed with porcine curiosity. Driven by questions – those silent, inner currents that move us, sentients, to know, grow, go farther. You can almost hear the irresistible question behind Lucas' every imperious action. And it's almost impossible not to want to know the answer. "What if I chase a horse?" "What if I bathe in the drinking water fountain?" "What if I push this baby stroller around, screaming baby and all?" "What if I break into the people house, tear open the feed bags and spread the feed around?" "What if I keep returning to the sounder that rejected me, time after time?" "What if I leave the skyless pit I was born into?" "What lies beyond its crushing cement walls?" "What if I pursue Petunia, the baddest, meanest pig around?" …And he throws himself into these questions, with total fearlessness, total abandon. The answer seems to be worth the risk or asking. It's not just moxie. It is an

explorer's personality, curiosity and cross.

Had he not escaped, he would have been caged, shoulder to shoulder, with thousands of other young captives like himself, fattened in the dark stench of a pig farm, crammed in a truck with dozens of other terrified victims, driven to the slaughterhouse in his final, frightened journey, and killed in cold blood, execution style: no hesitation, no mercy, no remorse.

Someone with Lucas' personality would have fought to his last breath. He would not have accepted his tragic life as inevitable. He would have struggled, scraped, screamed, expressed more vocally, and more visibly than others the absolute despair of being a suffering soul buried alive in a cement grave, condemned to a short, excremental existence, murdered for a taste. He would have lost.

By contrast, a docile pig like Oscar would have frozen in silent despair. He would have focused every bit of his energy on enduring, suffering, bearing the unbearable. He would have tried to accept, not challenge, the relentless misery inflicted on him. He would have spent his short time on earth like most farmed animals – taking the beatings and the mutilations, and the sunless hell of his existence, the way abused children take the abuse: as though it were deserved, as though the abuser's perverse pleasure were their only worth, and their only identity – without that, they are nothing.

Lucas is one of the few pigs in the world who is unscathed by the atrocities of farming. He's been free most of his life. Free to experience the world's terrible beauty on his own terms, and free to be increased by it, or crushed by it. Free to be deeply wounded and deeply healed. Free to grow from his own mistakes. Free to fall in love, and fall hard. He does.

He approaches Petunia, usually at dusk, when everybody is out, active, and eagerly anticipating dinner before the long night's rest. He is well aware of the danger – Petunia bit, boxed, bashed, pushed, plugged, punched, slammed, slugged and threw him down before. But he approaches her anyway.

He swaggers suavely towards her, snorts sweetly, tiptoes behind her, what's left of his tail, politely, submissively down, head bowed, eyes courteously averted. She either ignores him or scolds and spanks him. He comes back for more – nose in the breeze of her being, eyes half-closed, as though inhaling the rarest perfume, mouth parted in an ecstatic smile, and emitting a series of soft, gurgling whimpers to sweeten her mood, cooing in her ear like a dove – singing to her in languages that she may not understand but her heart may, will, must. And he, the unchallenged Bad-Bold-Beautiful-Bodacious Boy of the sanctuary, lowers his head, blinks shyly, and whimpers submissively when Petunia shoves him.

There is no mistaking that Lucas' stream of infatuated sounds at Petunia's side is a serenade of love, submission, supplication, seduction, scintillation. Nothing compares to Petunia, nothing distracts him from her. He follows her around while she is engrossed in foraging for tasty tidbits. She totally ignores him. He totally ignores her food finds. Even though he pretends to be interested in everything she uncovers, eats, and praises in low, contented grunts, he never even tries to touch any of those delicacies. It's just a way to get closer and stay closer longer, while she is

occupied with that morsel. It's not the food, it's the fact that their noses are on the same scent-length, and, while she is rapt in her found treat, she suffers his cheek touching hers.

This is where he wants to be. This is his hog heaven. He has a whole sanctuary, a whole world of freedom to explore – and he does – but what he craves most is the small, dangerous, mysterious world that unfolds only at Petunia's side. He loves her. She is his greatest, most burning question – one that you can almost hear behind his every suave move, and perhaps the only Lucas question you almost don't want to know the answer to. "Will you love me back?"

– Joanna Lucas

Sophie

Finding Our Way Together

From the time I started volunteering at the sanctuary, Sophie claimed a special place in my heart. Even more so than the other pigs, Sophie has always had lots of trouble walking. Her hips are stiff and her knees no longer bend. She walks by throwing one straight leg forward then the other. Still, she gets around the barn and the field and even goes out to the mud bath. And wherever Sophie is, if you call out to her, she will sit up, look right at you and grunt as if to say, "Hello, come see me, come over." She calls us to step over the fence, scratch behind her ears, rub her forehead.

Like Sophie, the other pigs are Hampshires, black with a white stripe across their shoulders. There are ten in the herd, all from the same rescue. They had come from a rodeo, where the plan was to force them into a greased pig chase, then slaughter and roast them as a grand finale.

I call the pigs a "herd" but it's more like a tribe. Once when Andy had to be restrained to get a shot of antibiotics, he screamed. All the other pigs came into the barn, grunting in rhythm. The sound reverberated so loudly against the walls we humans couldn't hear each other speak. The pigs grunted in duets or trios, snout to snout, their bellies heaving, and every deep grunt felt like it was going right down our spines. When Andy's shot was done, they all went about their business, back into the yard or to piles of straw.

Last year, the Hampshires turned eight, an old age for pigs bred to reach "market weight," namely slaughter weight, in six months. By eight years, they had grown way past market weight. For years, they'd lived with bodies that were too big for their bones, too big for their joints and tendons. With six- or seven-hundred-pound bodies balanced on tiny ballerina feet, all of our pigs have some difficulty walking. Stubby is the biggest; Cromwell snores when he sleeps and pins his ears back like he's flying; Zach limps some days but has good days where he's fine. And there's Oliver, who walks to breakfast and dinner with his tongue out; Louie who's quiet for a pig; Lodo who scared us all when he slipped and fell. We thought we'd need the tractor to get him up, but he stood and walked away like nothing so embarrassing as falling ever could have happened to him. And there's Wilbur, sweet and usually first into the feeding area – after Patsy and Judy of course.

Patsy and Judy are pink pigs who came to join the herd as teenagers. They tried to establish their position in the tight-knit tribe by singling out Sophie – the pig with the most trouble walking – and tormenting her. I used to try to sneak treats to Sophie, but that backfired around the pink pigs. Any treat Sophie got was a huge affront to them. They'd bite her legs and chase her around the barn. Or they'd walk up to her with a high-pitched squeal like some mean-girl threat of "I'm going to get you." Or they'd mount her when she was lying by the pond, throwing themselves diagonally across her back. They left the other two female Hampshires, Dharma and Dolly, more or less alone. Sophie suffered the brunt.

When not bothered by Patsy and Judy, Sophie, Dharma and Dolly, the three herd matrons, would lie nose to nose in the mud pool during the hot days or next to each other in the straw in the barn – just as they had for their whole lives. They ate together and slept together. They hung out with the boys, too, but they were a trio – from the potential rodeo-barbeque to eight years later, they were the old ladies at the sanctuary.

Dharma was sturdy on her feet and always made it to breakfast and dinner. Dolly was just wobbly. Walking for her was never point A to point B, more of a meandering from side to side.

Toward the end of one summer, Dolly was wobbling so much, that the sanctuary director sent her to the veterinary hospital at Cornell University. In surgery, the doctors found inoperable tumors on Dolly's spine that were not only throwing off her balance, but were most likely causing her a lot of pain as well. Dolly was euthanized under anesthesia.

And then there were just the two, Dharma and Sophie. And of course the two pink, Sophie-tormenting teens, Judy and Patsy.

A month after Dolly died, Dharma developed a tumor in her uterus, a common occurrence in female pigs. Veterinarians discovered the tumor had grown so close to her heart that it couldn't be removed. Dharma never made it back home;

she too was euthanized.

A few days after Dharma died, I went into the pig barn, calling out, "Soph! Sophie!" She sat up and grunted "hello" back. I stepped over the fence and knelt by her. She looked at me, like she always does, straight in the eye. The thought occurred to me that no one had told her – she didn't know. "Dharma's gone, Sophie," I said, "She's not coming back."

Sophie grunted and turned away from me, something she'd never done before. Then Judy came into the barn. She walked over to Sophie, snorting with her snout in the straw. I thought, "Great, Sophie loses her last, dearest friend and now the tormenting resumes." Judy put her pink nose against Sophie's, but she didn't bite her. Instead, she started arranging straw into a bed with her hoof. I stopped petting Sophie and sat back to watch.

Judy made her pile of straw then lay down next to Sophie, who was still turned away from me. Without hesitating, Sophie lifted her head and put it on Judy's pink shoulder. As I turned the lights out and closed the door to the barn, there they were, Sophie and Judy, going into the night, head to shoulder, snout to snout, heart to heart.

— *Jean Rhode*

Whitaker

Abbey

Heidi

Loretta

Eli

Harrison

Casey

Herbie　　　*Juliette*

Davi

44

Ralphie - Andy - Elvis
GENTLE GIANTS

Ralphie, Andy, and Elvis are adult male Holstein Steer. While in itself that might not sound so remarkable, male Holsteins are not a common sight. The reason for this is that they are an unwanted byproduct of the dairy industry and are killed for veal while they're still calves as they aren't milk producers and they aren't beef cows.

Receiving no consideration other than as units of monetary profit, Ralphie, Andy and Elvis were separated at birth from their mothers. They were rescued from dark, filthy barns, each tied to rails that wouldn't let them so much as turn around.

In terms of size, adult male Holsteins are monsters! Ralphie stands six feet tall (eight feet if he picks his head all the way up and taller still if one counts the horns). Once fully grown, they will stand even taller and will weigh slightly less than a Hyundai. Holsteins are huge animals and among the largest in the western hemisphere.

Ralphie, Andy, and Elvis each know exactly how powerful he is. Each knows his own physical size and each knows yours as well. Each is fully aware that he could cause you great damage. But that doesn't stop Ralphie from touching his nose to yours or letting you rub the vulnerable soft area under his two-foot long throat. And it doesn't stop Andy from licking your arm like a cat (complete with sandpaper tongue) or lowering his forehead close to yours so the two of you can get in some head-rubbing time. Elvis can be a bit more reserved. But, when approached, he too will lower his head, lick your hand and allow you to brush him until your arm gives out.

How often during your week do you encounter such power wrapped up in such gentleness?

— Bob Esposito

Charley

At Work

Charley created a vegetarian just last week. "You mean this is what they make beef out of?" asked Gretchen. She was brushing loose hair from Charley's massive side, as he tilted his head in an expression of pure ecstasy. "Yup, that would be right," I said. Charley's cuddly good looks (all 2,000 pounds of them) qualify him as an ambassador for large bovines even from a distance. His gentle and inquisitive personality touches you immediately and makes you wonder why anyone would think of such a character as a "food animal."

As people walk, drive, or ride their bikes down the winding country road that fronts on the pasture where Charley the ox lives with his horse friends, they often stop to visit. Charley obliges by lumbering over to the fence. His curiosity and friendliness show through as he sniffs and licks his visitors. Children reach to pat his large head with its curly golden locks of hair. With his one good eye (the other lost to an infection when he was a small calf) Charley takes in everything.

We met through the animal shelter in Tennessee where my wife was the veterinarian. Charley was found as a young calf, wandering and virtually blind in suburban Knoxville. He was never claimed. Unfortunately, intensive medical care was unable to save his infected eye, and adoptive homes for one-eyed oxen are not easy to come by. Since our house is a de facto home for the unadoptable, we felt that a pet ox would

fit in with the dogs, ducks, chickens, draft horses, bunnies, and turtles. So Charley came to live on our little farm in the hills east of town. We provided a calf stall and feed; he just provided himself, which was more than enough for us. His future roommates, Cass and Rheo, were huge rescued draft horses, and outweighed Charley by about 1,800 pounds each. However, coming from a particularly large breed of bovines, he soon matched the horses pound-for-pound.

As with all youngsters, Charley required a bit of education. Charley's first teacher was an eleven-year-old girl from France, who lived next door to our farm. Their friendship and rapport may have stemmed from the fact that Anais could actually pronounce Charley's breed – "Charolais" – properly. Charley learned how to wear a halter and lead, and he learned pretty quickly how much he loved to be brushed. It all came pretty naturally, as he always wanted to please.

When we moved to California, Charley, of course, came along. He traveled in a very large trailer with Cass and Rheo, and we stopped every night at fairgrounds in small towns across America. Gentle and well-behaved, Charley got out for a walk every few hours, just like our dogs. When, asked why we were moving with an ox, my answer would be: "we are friends for life."

Having long settled into his west coast routine, Charley starts each day by coming up to the feeding area to check the status of his breakfast. On the off chance that the humans are not out in the yard to feed by 7AM and some coaxing is required, the volume of his voice makes the whole valley ring. Though he spends most of his time in the pasture grazing, ruminating, and enjoying the central California sun, he is always available for an introduction to people who lack experience with the bovine ethos. Even when in deep sleep in his favorite grassy corner, his response to having his name called is immediate, yet he doesn't respond the way a dog or a human would. He doesn't see the call so much as a command as an invitation to a dialogue. And his response is generally, "Well, yes I'm here. What did you have in mind?" We go from there to consider whether haltering and a walk to the brushing area would be a good idea, or if some unrestrained grooming in the field would be more reasonable.

Going for a walk involves similar communication. Charley was well halter-trained from his youth, and his light rope halter is the only thing necessary for control, despite our weight disparity of a good ton. But there are often things along the route that might require his attention and scrutiny and I am compelled to oblige his interests. What is life if you don't take time to munch the poison oak anyway? At other times the important things require head up, ears forward, and a good alert snort. Giving me a tour of what he can sense and I cannot, and what attracts him that I miss, is Charley's contribution to my education. When I need reflection and calm there is really nothing better than walking with Charley.

Meandering down the old farm road, next to a creature who enjoys each moment for what it is, has taught me a good deal. With all that size and power there is never any use of force, only a desire to be "part of the herd" and have every

day be interesting and new. With the possibility of a good back scratch or quiet rumination always on the horizon, Charley sets an example for how we all might look at the world.

— *Eric Davis, DVM*

Justice

... For They Shall Be Comforted

Justice gazes at us calmly as we approach him in the field where he has chosen to sit for the afternoon. Actually, he doesn't just gaze at us ... he *looks* at us. He meets our eyes, and he holds them. There is a clear, obvious, recognizable intelligence in his eyes, and a look as if he intends to tell us something.

Michele, his caretaker, tells us his story:

"Justice was on the way to slaughter – a steer destined to be organic beef at the young age of a year-and-a-half – when he broke out of the truck and ran. What saved his life was a division of wildlife officer shooting him with a tranquilizer gun, making his "meat" unfit for human consumption due to the drugs now in his system. Otherwise, he would have been rounded up and re-trucked to the slaughterhouse.

When Justice first arrived at the sanctuary, he was so scared. The only other time he had been in a trailer was on the trip to the slaughterhouse, and so he had banged himself up terribly. That's how he broke his left horn – in that trailer banging around trying to get out of there. Sherman, another steer who lived at the sanctuary at that time, went over to him and started licking him through the fence and calmed him down. Justice has remembered that and

he's done it for every new arrival since.

Every time someone new comes it doesn't matter what species they are – goat, sheep, turkey, whatever – he knows if they're really scared. Like when

Rowdy, one of the sheep, got here, he was so scared. He was shaking so hard in the trailer, the whole thing was shaking. Rowdy was just screaming his head off, and here comes Justice, charging up the hill to help him. Justice, he hates livestock trailers.

We start new arrivals off in the chicken yard because it's safely enclosed, but they still have a 360 degree view of what's going on at the sanctuary. So we got Rowdy into the yard, and he was running around making lots of noise, and Justice came and just stood right next to the fence, on the other side. All the goats came up to see who the new guy was and Justice could tell that was making Rowdy nervous, so he turned around and took a couple of steps toward the goats, as if he was saying: "guys, just stand back a minute – you can look but you're a little too much right now," and they backed off.

Then Justice returned to this position up against the fence and Rowdy came over to him, although he'd never even seen cattle before. He stood right next to Justice, on the other side of the fence, and he stopped crying. They spent the entire night standing side by side. I took food and water over there, and they really didn't touch it, but Justice stayed on that side of the fence all night long. He stayed next to him and the next morning Rowdy was okay.

Justice did that for the llamas when they got here. He's so good. When the new guys come in, Justice just goes up to them and immediately calms them down, and I know it's because Sherman did that for him.

Even when the sick ones come here, and the only thing they're going to be able to do is die here but die in peace, as much peace as they possibly can have,

even if they never get to the point where they trust us humans, they pick up on the vibes of the other animals. They pick up on the peace, and Justice is one who really gives them that.

The best thing we can do is stand back. They know how to handle it. We're just humans. I learn something new from these guys every day and then as soon as I realize that I've learned it, it occurs to me, why didn't I know that? Why should this be some epiphany? They know so much more than we do."

Maybe what we see in Justice's eyes is *compassion*.

— *Diane Leigh*

Linda & Tricia

BBFF

Linda arrived at our shelter in upstate New York with twisted back legs and feet and a stiff gait caused by a broken pelvis which had never been treated when she was a calf. After many diagnostic tests, surgeons at the Cornell University Hospital for Animals determined that no procedure could reverse the damage to Linda's body, and that any additional trauma to her hips or back could cause further harm and even full paralysis. Because of this, Linda's doctors recommended that she live with our sheep rather than the cattle who, as they are generally larger than Linda, could easily injure her by accident. Fortunately, Linda lived very happily among sheep and goats, though it was clear that she still desired to mix with the cattle who daily mooed back and forth with her from a few barns away. Linda's wish eventually came true, however, with the arrival of a special cow named Tricia.

We received a call from a former dairy farmer desperately seeking help for a special needs animal. She explained that when she left the cooperative dairy she was part of, she took Tricia, a blind cow she had raised from a calf, and moved her to another farm, hoping to keep her safe from harm. But the farmer at that farm, who agreed to take Tricia in, continued to breed her. After Tricia gave birth to a son (a "byproduct" of no use to the dairy industry), the farmer decided that she was not worth the extra work it took to care for her and planned to send her to slaughter. The woman discovered this plan and convinced the farmer to spare Tricia, if she

could find another home quickly. That's when she contacted us. She begged us to take Tricia in and we agreed, knowing that we could provide the special care and environment she would need.

When Tricia arrived at the shelter, she not only turned out to be the tiniest cow we had ever seen, but was also so distraught that she spent her first day mooing loudly and circling her pen. When we could not console Tricia after her first 24 hours at the sanctuary, I called the woman who had asked for our help to see if she had seen Tricia act like this before. Tragically, she revealed to me then that Tricia's calf had only recently been taken to slaughter, and the poor cow's distress suddenly made all the sense in the world: Tricia was clearly still mourning the loss of her son.

We quickly vaccinated and de-wormed her and made sure she was healthy so we could introduce her to Linda as soon as possible. After all, the two seemed like they would be a perfect match since Tricia was so small and would pose no danger to Linda. When the two met, Tricia was beside herself with joy and spent hours licking Linda over and over again. At first, Linda was a little bit apprehensive since she had never lived with other cows, but within a few hours, she was licking Tricia right back.

Now the two of them are inseparable. Tricia spends her days lying in the straw, licking her pal until she is practically

soaking wet. She no longer cries out or moves in circles — the only exception being if she is separated from Linda for even a moment (in which case Linda cries out too). Looking at them together, it is clear that these sensitive and sweet animals needed each other to be completely fulfilled — and it's as if Tricia came here not only so that her own life could be saved, but also so that she could give Linda a second chance for true happiness. They are a perfect example of the power of love and cow kisses, and we just know that they'll be BBFFs (Best Bovine Friends Forever).

— *Susie Coston*

Sammy

Rochester

Helen

Hannah

Boone, Alphonso & Hersche

Aubrey

Jewle

Melvin

Sun Day

Melvin has been strutting up and down the hallway since dawn, hoisting his enormous body across the 20 step stretch from the kitchen to the front door where he lingers, swaying unsteadily from side to side like a tower of mismatched dishes, gazing expectantly into the driveway, trilling sweet things at it, puffing his chest, arching his wings, looking for something, waiting, stirring, shimmering, shuffling his feet…. After a while, he turns around slowly, laboriously, toilsomely, and drags himself back to the kitchen, heaving, and wheezing and staggering on gouty legs, then embarks again on the arduous, 20 step trek to the front door, parading in full celebration gear, big as a carnival float and as jubilantly bedecked as one.

It's Sunday. At least that's what our calendars say – Sunday, the cusp of a new week – but, to Melvin, in Melvin's sense of time, it's something else, something brighter and luckier.

He was rescued from a local flesh farm and brought to the sanctuary with his five brothers when they were all very young, barely four months old, still soft in their feathers and tender in their voices – 6 newborn planets wobbling in their axes, orbiting the grasslands and the ferns with a buoyancy in their round, befeathered selves that almost felt like laughter – and, for a brief time after their arrival at the sanctuary, that first spring, summer and fall of freedom, they were grounded so firmly in the hope of things, the wings of things, the rapture of things, the giddy promise of things, the endless summer of things, that they seemed inextinguishable – six new suns, shining the warmth of their attention towards everything in their world with such constancy, such enthusiasm, such intensity, that it felt like love.

Everything they could see, smell, touch, taste, hear was embraced as nothing less than an earthly delight: the salty-mossy-fruity-fenny-bitter-acrid-sweet scents of grasses, the hedgerows, and the grasslands, and the bogs, the ravishing rain, the mud-luscious puddles, the iridescent hues of feathers and of snow, the sap-oozing milkweeds, the languidly stretched fields, the knotted thickets of bramble, the sweet, sapid, scintillating sights, scents, sounds of life all around them, the very dirt under their feet, and everyone walking on it. But almost as soon as they entered this welcoming world, it started

to ebb away from them. Imperceptibly at first, but then faster and faster, harder and harder, punishing them where it had rewarded, pummeling them where it had caressed.

As Melvin, George, Stanley, Alfred, Elmer and Archie became progressively crippled, their genetically manipulated bodies growing around them like tumors, engulfing them in their grip, crushing themselves under their own weight, suffocating, choking, destroying themselves in the name of our "turkey dinners," their ability to participate in life diminished and, with it, so did their openness to its gifts. Their daily cavalcades into the open fields became slower and slower, shorter and shorter, fewer and fewer, and then, eventually, not at all: George, Stanley, Alfred, Elmer and Archie died one by one, and, with each of them, a whole world of consciousness, memories, yearnings, everything each of them knew and remembered ceased to exist with him, the face of each, the scent of his body, his enthusiasm, his intelligence was gone with him.

After each loss, Melvin's own light dimmed, as if disconnected from a power source. And, as the burden of sorrows, ailments and age accumulated, it took him longer and longer to return to bold, brilliant, demanding life.

But he always did. He lifted himself from sadnesses that grew deeper and deeper with each new loss, and he embarked again on his long, burning journeys all the way from his barn to the trailer, where the visitors were, and resumed the bruising, exhilarating toil of following them around, wheezing and coughing, his lungs and heart barely keeping up with his giant body, his legs deformed under its weight. He dragged himself back to the world he loved – improbable and sublime, like a house on legs, like a ship on dry sand –

and savored each of its dwindling gifts: straw-scented shade, sweet grass and cracked corn, Shylo's friendship, Chris' voice, Michele's presence, visitors he had charmed, and visitors he had yet to enchant. And he loved life with all her faults, and forgave her many trespasses.

Then, one day, he did not. When Shylo, his last remaining friend died, he isolated himself in the back of the barn and refused to leave. Morning after morning, the gates would fling open and everyone would rush out to greet the day, but Melvin did not. He remained rooted in the same dark spot and refused to leave. He did not move, he did not turn, he did not look away from the wall.

Day after day, we'd find him in the same secluded nook, alone, listless, expecting nothing, demanding nothing, taking everything without joy, interest or protest, as though it was all happening to someone else. And nothing, not the promise of treats, nor the presence of visitors, nor any of the things he had so relished, could make him want to leave his self-imposed exile. If we hadn't physically carried him outside, he would have remained in exactly the same spot, staring at the wall in front of him from morning till night, his back turned to the world he had so loved.

He shut the world out with such finality that he seemed more crushingly, more irrevocably gone than Shylo himself. That mysterious something that had resurrected him before, that obscure and irrepressible something that had restored his great broken heart so many times before, seemed irretrievable now. His body slumped, his eyes drained of light, his spirit wilted. He stopped preening, he stopped communicating, he stopped showering the world with his rapt attention, he stood there silent and still, anchored in place by a sort of strange devotion, as if waiting for something, an end or a return. When the weather turned cold, we brought him inside the house. And that's where he still is today, sharing his shriveled world with the shut-ins, the frail, the old, the ill, the crippled who are there for a while or for the rest of their lives. Not much has changed. Despite the constant care and attention, he is still withdrawn, still solitary, still uncommunicative, still reluctant to move.

Except on Sundays.

On Sundays, he stirs before everyone else, aflutter with his old excitement, anticipating something good, and already singing to this good thing, strutting for it, trilling turkey tunes to it — a big, crippled bird, dancing for joy when he can barely walk, trumpeting for joy when he can barely breathe. Acting as if the lost world of green fields, endless summers, thriving tribe of turkey toms was there again, swaggering about the room with laughter about him, displaying his plumage in a magnificent show of glistening feathers, hoisting his aching body across the room, dragging himself on swollen joints, covering the 20 long, painful steps from the kitchen to the front door, waiting, stirring, shimmering, shuffling his feet, atwitter with expectation, until he finally hears the sound he's been waiting for: Ruth's car pulling into the driveway.

Then he kicks the door with his left foot and demands something he vehemently rejects the rest of the time: to go out. We open the door and he swaggers out in the yard in full parade gear, his wattle quickened scarlet, his tail fanned out like a triumphal chariot wheel, his neck arched like a rainbow, his wings stretched all the way to the ground and held taut with robust, muscular grace. Ruth is here! And he acts as though the miraculous, spellbinding, rapturous days of his youth are back again, alive and present with the rich, red pulse of life — not remembered like a story, but felt, known, believed like a scent, like bread baking. Ruth is here!

And he follows her around, quivering and shaking on gouty legs, and issuing forth a most astonishing array of flowing sounds punctuated by percussive feather pops in the tips of his wings, his burdened heart all aglow, his lungs filled not with mere oxygen but with something else, something imperious, something invincible, a force, not a substance — a shot of livingness straight into the throbbing heart with all its folly, wisdom, ache and yearning to be nothing but loved.

By evening, Ruth, has come and gone for another week and Melvin is still abuzz, ablaze, abloom with the swarm of the day, and relives it well into the night. Of all the people he sees every day, of all the souls he shares the house with, of all the volunteers gracing the sanctuary every week, only Ruth sweetens his heart till it remembers life's most beautiful song — is! is! is!

— Joanna Lucas

Amelia

GENTLE COMPANION

On a perfect spring day I drove to the Virginia Eastern Shore to visit a sanctuary dedicated to the rescue and care of poultry. After I arrived, Karen, the sanctuary's founder, and I spoke at length, sitting in various spots around the yard. While most of the residents went about their business, there were a few birds almost constantly in my peripheral vision. There was Frankincense, the peacock, who was constantly flaring his tail for attention; the vain and glorious rooster Rhubarb; Aubrey, a young male turkey who had a bit of spring fever; and Amelia, a quiet white turkey, who hovered nearby watching. She was more curious about what I was doing and left all the preening and posturing to the males in the yard.

Aubrey and Amelia came to live at the sanctuary when they were about five months old. Maryland and Virginia's Eastern Shore are to poultry farming what Midwest feedlots are to cattle. Aubrey and Amelia are descended from birds specifically bred for consumption.

After we finished talking, Karen left me to get to know the birds and photograph them. Amelia would creep closer and closer to me and get very still when I turned to pay her attention. Everywhere I went in the yard, she was never far behind. She reminded me of the dogs I share my life with — they always have to be wherever I am.

Amelia spends most of her time with the hens and roosters, but she is also rather independent. She enjoys human companionship and seeks out physical affection from visitors and volunteers. She loves spaghetti, as do most of the birds. She and the chickens often dust bathe together and then find some sunshine in which to relax.

She continued to watch me, shadowing my moves in the yard. The inherent curiosity of these gentle birds is what almost wiped them out when Europeans arrived in North America. They would inquisitively walk up to people and were shot in droves. Their guilelessness was derided and to this day "turkey" is used as an insult.

Eventually I had no choice but to simply give Amelia a hug, which she seemed to enjoy. I held the camera out and took a photo of the two of us together. I wanted to capture her sweetness and desire to be cuddled.

Since that day, I've met more birds, some with huge personalities, but in thinking about them all, Amelia's sweetness keeps tugging at me. Her simple desire to be hugged is what punches me in the gut when I walk past the deli section at the grocery store.

— *Davida Gypsy Breier*

Ariala & Rhosyln
Beating the Odds

Well-groomed, well-nourished, with every beautiful white feather in place, sisters Ariala and Rhoslyn are a handsome pair. Inquisitive and quirky, they strut and peck around their home in northern California seemingly unaware of the horrific and heartbreaking events that brought them there or the harrowing fate they avoided.

When Ariala and Rhoslyn were scarcely hatched, they and 15,000 of their brethren were packed tightly into storage containers and flown from Detroit to a turkey breeding facility in California. Most of them never made it. On that hot July day, more than 13,000 baby turkeys suffocated while their airplane was delayed on a scorching Las Vegas runway. By the time the plane landed in San Francisco, most had died. While 1,900 of the survivors were sent to their final destination to become "breeders" whose offspring would be sold for food, Ariala and Rhoslyn were among 11 baby turkeys pulled from among the mass of carcasses by the local humane society and turned over to an animal rescue group with a sanctuary in the area.

The sisters flourished and grew quickly, as domestic turkeys are bred to do. By early November they were ready to make one more trip, this time to a small town south of San Francisco where they were adopted by Karen and Mike, who opened their hearts and home to them. Now the girls spend their days in the garden, surveying the goings-on, getting into mischief and chirping their comments to Karen and Mike as they follow them around the yard.

The girls also serve as living lessons to the many children who visit the farm. Their excitement at having visitors shows as they fluff up their fancy tail feathers, chirping loudly and prancing about to show everyone that these erstwhile "Thanksgiving dinners" are actually social, friendly and curious.

These two lovely birds, if given the choice, would rather sit by the side of a human being for companionship than forage and peck like their chicken sisters. They prefer to watch and listen; their curious natures lead them on treks across the garden to the side of the house where they peek in on Mike and Karen through the glass doors. They even try to sneak into the house if no one is looking! Ariala loves it when Karen kisses her on the top of the head. She goes into a trance and sinks down so Karen can rub under the mesmerized turkey's wings.

Not everything is rosy for the girls, even now, however. After decades of selective breeding, domestic turkeys are vastly different from their wild cousins. These birds fatten up quickly, especially in their exaggeratedly-broad breast region. This "front-loading" makes them so top-heavy that, even with their expansive wingspread, they will never fly. Grounded for life and still overbalanced, their walking gait is ungainly at best. As breeders don't want or expect their turkeys to live very long, no one has ever bothered to breed stronger legs and feet to carry the disproportionately-burdened birds. Imagine an obese pigeon supported by a sparrow's legs. Karen and Michael have to monitor the girls' diets because even a little overindulgence can mean premature crippling or broken bones. As it is, even in their lovely garden with doting parents, the lifespan of Ariala and Rhoslyn will be short.

But for now, living free on a farm of their own, surrounded by stately redwoods and gnarled live oak trees, Ariala and Rhoslyn are the recipients of the greatest gift human beings can give: compassion. Rescuing, feeding, nurturing, adopting, loving – all these modest acts of kindness have brought the sisters' lives back from the brink of the squalid future they had in store for them. These bright, impish birds have beaten the odds.

— *Kit Salisbury*

Annie

Molly

Jordan

Swoozie

Simon

Paloma

Tanya & Raposal

Hal

Olivia

TEACH YOUR CHILDREN

Olivia arrived at the sanctuary several years ago when she was abandoned by a family, who, having lost their home to a fire, simply picked up and moved away. One of the first residents of the sanctuary, Olivia would make her daily farm rounds which included grass grazing, catching up with staff members, taking naps, plundering any feed left unsecured, and hanging out by the chicken yard where she could view nearly the entire farm. This was Olivia's new life in her new home at the sanctuary.

But what no one knew was that Olivia was also a sap for lost souls.

Dylan came to the farm, a shaky-legged, malnourished calf who had been forcibly taken from his mother at birth just one week earlier to be raised for veal. Though humans were now fawning over him, he was a scared little dude on unfamiliar land and without a single animal friend. Poking around the farm, Dylan explored his new home and quickly discovered Olivia. He needed a friend, and though Olivia didn't appear to need a silly calf to accompany her on her daily rounds, she accepted Dylan loping along beside her and the two quickly became both field-mates and pen-mates. Olivia didn't have to alter her day in anyway for Dylan, she just had to be herself and make her daily farm rounds. Olivia knew where to eat, where to drink, where to rest, which humans to mooch treats from, and which feed cans to raid for the choicest payout. By observing Olivia, Dylan gained

knowledge of the farm and also built a sense of himself. Through Olivia's example, Dylan could feel assured that he was in a place where there was not a lot of reason to fear and where there was a lot of reason to just be a calf.

Over the coming months, Dylan and Olivia went everywhere and did everything together. If you visited the farm during that period, together they would come meet you for introductions. If you had apples or carrots in your pockets you were given immediate entrée. If you did not have apples or carrots in your pockets you were still given immediate entrée but they would check in with you later in case you had acquired any in the interim.

After more than a year of roaming the farm together, it was time for the now much larger Dylan to join the adult steer in the steer field. With knowledge of the farm and confidence in himself provided by his days with Olivia, Dylan fit in seamlessly with his new bovine field-mates. Dylan knew how to be a steer and he learned it, in great part, from a goat. Olivia and Dylan would maintain ongoing contact with each other by grazing the steer field fence line together until they'd drift apart to continue their now separate daily farm routines.

Soon after Dylan joined the other steer, Albie the goat arrived at the sanctuary. He had been found roaming a park in Brooklyn. Young Albie was only a few months old and displayed signs of having been hog-tied which caused injuries that turned one of his front legs gangrenous. As with Dylan, Albie sought out Olivia's company in his new environment. And also as with Dylan, Olivia accepted Albie's company on her daily rounds and the two became fast teacher-student-buds. Part of Albie's gangrenous leg eventually had to be amputated but nothing could keep Albie from following Olivia as she went through her day. Olivia walked; Albie hobbled. Walk-hobble-graze, walk-hobble-drink, walk-hobble-snooze, walk-hobble-burgle all unguarded goat feed.

Olivia was an orphan magnet. As sure as the sun rose in the morning, newly arrived animals would seek out Olivia's company and she never turned away a soul. Through Olivia, each new arrival would gain knowledge of the farm and the confidence to feel safe in their new home. Olivia never sought the company of a new arrival but she never refused to accept those who found her. Did Olivia benefit in some way from these relationships? She never gave any hints, she just went about her day.

In 2007, Olivia was diagnosed with lymphoma, and that winter lost her ability to stand or to walk. She was set up comfortably in the barn for several weeks before moving into the farm director's house. Many at the sanctuary believed that she would never return to the barn. The inability to stand can be a sign that the end is near.

Though Olivia could not stand or walk her wits never dulled and her appetite never diminished. She continued to accept smushes from anyone passing by and she could still mooch the food out of your hand before you knew it was gone. People were now coming to the farm just to see Olivia and to sit with her and talk. People always talked with Olivia, probably because Olivia always answered. Olivia spoke with her eyes and you always knew where both of you stood. Even in her weakened condition Olivia knew who you were and she knew who she was; anything else just fell away as not important enough for conversation.

Towards the end of winter, Olivia unexpectedly began trying

to stand. Two or three minutes at a time was all she could muster but it was enough to overjoy her fans with the hope that she might be getting better. Soon after, she began to take a few steps at a time. Often she'd crumple a bit but she would again rise and take more steps. This standing-walking-crumpling-standing-walking kept up for several weeks until the crumpling disappeared and she was able go outside with staff for short walks. After several more weeks of gradually longer walks, Olivia returned to the barn and to those farm animals who continued to seek out her company. No one could have predicted Olivia would regain her mobility and no one was left untouched by her recovery.

Olivia was back to her daily farm routine and over the coming months she continued to accept the various newcomers who sought her company. Clover, the goat who was found alone in an alley with her umbilical cord still attached, and Felix, the lamb who lost a portion of his leg to a predator, both received their farm education from Olivia. Together, Olivia, Albie, Clover and Felix became a formidable grazing gang and feed-can-theft mob.

When Olivia passed away the next October the humans at the farm took it hard. That's what humans do when they lose a friend. How the animals took it is known best to them. But if you ever come to the sanctuary, you'll see what Olivia left behind. You'll see it in the younger farm animals she befriended and nurtured who are now integral members of their respective pastures. And if you mention Olivia's name to the staff, volunteers or visitors who spent their own special moments with Olivia, you'll see it in their faces.

— *Bob Esposito*

Jeremy & Lenny
The Destiny of a Toddler

Lenny got my attention first – how could he not? – he was prancing on the roof of my car. When I stopped laughing and wondered if my insurance would cover "Act of Goat" I walked over and introduced myself. He was having a fine time using the car's height to reach the lowest boughs of a tree. I climbed up and gently removed him. The minute his hooves hit the dirt he ran around the car, jumped on the hood, and resumed his playful grazing. Once again I clambered onto the car and scooped him up, but now wise to his tricks I was unsure of what to do with the naughty young goat.

As I carried Lenny into the pasture I was struck by how much like my own toddler he was acting. Lenny even weighed about the same. His writhing protestations, despite knowing he wouldn't get his own way this time, were exactly that of my two-year-old son. Lenny's brother, Jeremy, was coaxed into the field by fellow visitors. Terry, the sanctuary's co-founder, called to him and he came running to her. In his run there was evident joy, so full of unnecessary movement and silliness. Again, I saw my son and his silly walks. I could see in an instant that Jeremy possessed a sweetness and desire to be mothered. Lenny, on the other hand, was full of mischief and already seeking his independence.

We put them into the barn, Jeremy listening and complying and Lenny attempting to bolt out the door. I have the same problem with our kitchen door, which is kept shut with a bungee cord after too many escapes by my toddler into the yard.

When Jeremy and Lenny came back out that afternoon, they were all over Terry. The unbridled physical love of a toddler is all about tormenting, mauling, and snuggling… all at the same time.

Leaving Terry's lap, they chased the chickens for amusement. The chickens would run from them, unlike their elder goats who only offered stoic glares in response to their pestering. So often I have similar antics to contend with in my own house, but there my son tries to chase the cats and dogs, who are about as amused as the chickens and elder goats.

Later, after I moved my car out from under the tree, they found the tractor. For whatever reason, little boys love tractors and little boy goats are no different. They perched and climbed all over it, much as my son would have done had he been there.

Every mother thinks about her child's destiny. Jeremy and Lenny's original destiny would have cut their lives short when they were about four months old, still just babies. They were born on a small farm that produced goat cheese. The only reason for their birth was to keep their mother producing milk and they were taken away before she could even know them. Born male, they only held value to the farmer as meat. Instead, someone intervened on their behalf, changing that destiny. Their mother will never know what happened to her boys, but they are safe, comfortable and loved, which is all any of us ever hope for our children.

— *Davida Gypsy Breier*

Georgie

Ray-Ray

Wendy, Ady & Colvin

Doris

Devlin

Ewegenia

Daisy, Adam, Dorothy & Hickory

Lucky Lady

LESSONS LEARNED

Sweet Lucky Lady, one of the many animals rescued from New York City through the years, arrived at the sanctuary with a deeply-rooted fear of humans. Like many farm animals saved from the city's live animal markets – places where animals are sold to customers for a few dollars apiece and slaughtered on site – this timid ewe backed into corners or took refuge among flock-mates to get away from people, even those who were bringing her feed. She had been torn from her mother's side; hauled off to the city where she was yelled at, poked, prodded, and stuck in a pen with other terrorized animals then pursued through the Bronx after she narrowly escaped slaughter. Who could blame her for being scared?

Even so, it seems that time can sometimes heal all wounds, and after more than a year spent getting acquainted with people from a distance, Lucky Lady is not quite so shy anymore. In fact, following caregivers around while they are distributing medications and stealing a quick nose-to-nose nuzzle with her pals is now a daily routine for Lucky. And, where once you needed a telephoto lens to take her photo, she is now always right there to strike a pose when you pull out a camera. The change has been remarkable, and it is clear when you look at Lucky that she is finally at ease and feels very secure in her new life.

Like most animals who come to our sanctuary, Lucky Lady seems to realize that she is loved and has nothing more to

fear. When animals like her can let go and trust again it makes you stop and think about how often we humans choose not to forgive. We close ourselves off from those who commit even minor infractions against us, which are nothing in comparison to what animals like Lucky experience every day. Seeing this incredible sheep's intense fear replaced with acceptance and love gives me hope that we all have the capacity to heal and forgive, if only we can open our hearts to the good in the world.

– *Susie Coston*

Marcie

Portrait of a Beautiful Soul

When Marcie arrived at Peaceful Prairie Sanctuary, she had already lost everything – her freedom, her community, her family, her youth, every baby she had ever had, everyone she had ever loved, everyone she had ever trusted, everything that was familiar.

She arrived in this new world with nothing except – for the brief time before she went blind – the ability to see with her own eyes this improbable land of open vistas, big sky, free inhabitants and people who wished them life, this Free State that billions of captive animals never experience but that all yearn for in their living cells to their last breath. And perhaps to believe it. Like all farmed animals, Marcie was defined not by what was there, but by what was missing – the visible and invisible amputations of a lifetime of slavery – mutilated body, broken spirit, wounded soul, unrealized life, unrealized potential, capacity for pain filled to the brim, capacity for joy left utterly empty. In her years of confinement on a small family farm, where she repeatedly watched her babies being killed, so much had already been taken from her that, by the time she was rescued and brought to a place where she could finally begin her life, there wasn't much left to build a life on. Her first year at

the sanctuary, when she could still see, she fled from anyone who looked like her abusers – any human being around – and, for the rest of her life, she avoided anyone who looked like herself – every ewe, ram or lamb around. She "hid" her big, beautiful, billowy self among the goats, dawdling along conspicuously ovine amid the gust of quick, slender, angular, light-footed goats, secure in the belief that she was well camouflaged among these creatures who looked, walked, sounded, and acted nothing like herself. She traveled with them, foraged with them, camped with them, ignored the fact that, to everybody's mind but her own, they were a poor fit for her – too fast, too rowdy, too mischievous, too bold, too unpredictable for her – and forgave them their many trespasses such as the times when they left her behind, way out in the field, ignored her calls for location, and went home without her. But, for reasons she well understood, she remained unflinchingly loyal to them for the rest of her life. Whatever Marcie saw in the goats, learned from them, received from them was clearly something she needed. We joked that she thought she was a goat. But, more likely, the opposite was true: what seemed to draw her to the goats was not the imagined similarity but the perceived difference. She seemed to want to be someone completely unlike herself, a different animal altogether, someone totally unlike the powerless victim she had been all her life.

So she joined the goats and shared her deepest moments of peace with them. You could see her and them resting in the sun, in a trance-like almost solemn state, as though listening together to a magnificent symphony and in fact doing just that: "hearing the leaves of spring, the rustle of insect wings, the wind darting over the face of the pond," and savoring the scent of the wind itself, feeling beauty, being absorbed by beauty – not what WE call beauty, not the pretty things – but what IS beauty: the knowledge inherent in all things, in a stone, a leaf, a blade of grass, the profound experience of harmony and connection with something deeply good and deeply loving, the felt wisdom of being alive in a world of scent, and taste, and sound, and touch, with nerve endings responding in delight to every breeze, every faint happening, every detail in the world's face of dazzling color and rolling movement and depth.

Those moments – full of feeling, brimming with exquisite awareness, giddy with the life within – she shared with the goats. But in her moments of sorrow she was alone. And she had moments of wrenching, inconsolable sorrow, some triggered by invisible quakes, others triggered by events that even we could see and understand, such as the times when the smell of lambs born, torn from their mothers and slaughtered on neighboring farms filled the air and stirred her old pain, a pain that didn't lessen with time but seemed to grow new thorns every spring. Those were the times when she wandered off most often, becoming separated from her adopted herd, getting lost and, in her blindness, unable to find her way home. Because human presence terrified her, the only way we could guide her back home was to call out to the goats hoping that they would respond loud enough for Marcie to hear and follow the sound trail back to the herd. The goats, she trusted, but humans evoked nothing but horror – the horror she remembered and the horror she anticipated at our hands.

We understood her apprehension and went out of our way to not intrude in her safe zone. What we didn't understand then and still don't fully understand today is why she chose to narrow the physical and emotional distance between us and got one inch closer to us every day until there was no distance left at all, until our noses touched, literally. She got nothing extra from our proximity. Nothing that she didn't already get in abundance while avoiding us – food, shelter, friends, treats were all readily available to her whether or not she accepted us. So why did she decide to trust us when, throughout her life, humans had done unspeakably cruel things to her for a taste of her babies' flesh, for a handful of wool, for a patch of lamb skin? Why did she suffer with us when she could just as easily ignore us?

It's hard to say. But the fact is, she not only accepted us, she sought us out. If, in her estimation, either of us had been inside the house too long, she knocked on the door with her hoof and summoned us out. We came out every time, treat in hand – because that's what we assumed she wanted. And, for the rest of her life, she "drilled" us out on the porch this way several times a day. Then, her last year with us, she extended her vigils into the night. She started to wait up for Chris, stationing herself on the porch, waiting quietly, patiently, as long as it took – until midnight, until the following morning, until

Chris was safely home from work. She waited without complaining, without asking for treats, or attention, or companionship, or any of the pleasures that we thought motivated her to knock on the door every afternoon. She just anchored herself at the front door and kept her late night, solitary vigils away from the security of the herd, away from shelter, under the open sky. And nothing could get her to move – neither Bluto's boisterous barking, nor the alarming distance from her goats, nor the rain, nor the thunder, nor the snow. She stood there like a good mother, wedged between earth and sky, with a mixture of courage, trust, expectation, hope and resignation, her massive body firmly anchored between the big, bad, perilous world and her self appointed charge, and she didn't budge until Chris was safely home. Only then would she finally get up, leave the porch and amble to her barn for the night, with the treat of solid proof that both Chris and Michele were alive and well.

It wasn't a "plan." It was a far simpler, far wiser, far more deeply felt truth than that. Marcie wished us life. She wanted for those she loved to continue to live and she was determined that, for once in her life, they would. She demanded treat-in-hand proof of our wellness several times every day, and she guarded the porch at night until she was sure that both of her humans were alive and well. It was simple enough. Most of us can understand love. What most of us may never understand is how Marcie could forgive her abusers so completely that she was able to love their kin.

— *Joanna Lucas*

Cebolla

Burke

Dot-Dash

Arnold

Sailor

Julep

Fiona, Harley & Cornwall

Huey, Duey & Sidekick Chick

Delilah, Elijah,
Harvey & Travis

Dutch

A Duck's Best Friend

Like humans, farm animals thrive on the companionship of good friends. They enjoy having someone by their side while they are dust bathing, wallowing in a mud hole, or even taking an afternoon snooze. Some of the strongest friendships I've seen are between male ducks. Most of them were rescued separately, so they did not form these bonds while experiencing the cruelties of the world together. Rather, they met at the sanctuary, where they purposefully sought each other out, seeing in one another a kindred spirit and forming an impenetrable bond. One of these loyal ducks is Dutch, a devoted companion to several birds through the years.

Dutch arrived a few years after his first best friend Rain's arrival. Their friendship began when they moved to the retirement area for ducks and geese, as both had arthritis and needed to live in a calm environment. Their bond quickly strengthened as they swam next to each other in their private pond and cuddled in the straw at night. When Dutch left the hutch in the morning, he always waited patiently for Rain to exit before he moved on; there was nothing that one did without the other. Even when Rain later developed cancer and made frequent trips to the vet, Dutch always waited eagerly for him to return, happily quacking "hello" at the first sight of his friend. The pair remained inseparable for years until Rain's health declined and Dutch had to say a final goodbye to his constant friend.

After Rain's death, Dutch continued with his daily routine of swimming in the pond and sunning in the grass with the older geese, but he obviously missed his friend terribly. Happily, Simon entered his world several months later and filled him with joy once again. When he arrived at the shelter, Simon was suffering from a joint infection and poor feather condition, but as his health improved, he began to enjoy taking daily swims. It was during these swims that Dutch befriended Simon and the two began floating on the water side by side. As he did with Rain, Dutch happily slowed down for Simon, waiting for his friend in the morning and night so they could walk back and forth from the pond to the hutch together. They never missed a moment of each other's company until Simon passed away, leaving Dutch on his own once again. Though heartbreakingly short, the time these boys shared as friends was truly special and cherished by both until the end.

Fortunately, sweet Dutch has proven to be quite a trooper and has not abandoned his kindly ways. Today Dutch's companions include Boris and Harry. Although they have been longtime friends, Dutch is beginning to win them over with his charm — kind of like a little brother who is hoping to hang out with the older, cooler crowd. When Harry and Boris ultimately accept him, they will have a friend for life, as Dutch is a loyal, accepting companion with a heart that remains open despite the great losses in his past.

— *Leanne Cronquist*

Goosifer

THE GOOSE FORMERLY KNOWN AS LUCIFER

He's easy to spot. He's the cranky, crabby, cantankerous, contentious, contrary, quarrelsome, crazy sonofagoose who "occupied" a corner of the pond yard, appropriated its assets – a broken wheelbarrow, an igloo, and a kiddy pool – hasn't left their side since, and will hiss, honk and spit at anyone who approaches them.

He is the goose who does ungoosly things – he will not swim, he will not socialize, he will not explore the world outside his tiny and separate world. Which is why the name Lucifer seemed appropriate – a rebel, a proud recluse, a tormented soul. But he is also the goose who "rides" pigs out of his yard by biting down on their tails, bracing his feet against their ample rumps, and spanking them with his wings until they're banished to the other side of the gate. Which is why we call him Goosifer. Goosifer grew up in a cage. As a youngster, his only contact was with Shylo, the turkey, and the man who "owned" them both. Without a community to teach him the rules, language and myths of his own species; without a family to teach him the strength and skills that living requires, he never learned how to exist fully and meaningfully in the world as a goose.

So Goosifer spends his days patrolling and protecting the borders of his solitary world, keeping all intruders safely out, and himself safely in, unless JC, the African goose comes calling. Then, with JC as a guide, he may leave his post and venture out for a brief outing. The two of them walk the open fields, harass innocent bystanders, honk, taunt, tease, trash-talk, and generally make great merriment and melody together. At the end of the excursion, JC brings Goosifer back to the gate and they part company. JC returns to his cross-species socializing. Goosifer returns to his solitary gatekeeping. It's as though he is defending a nest full of precious eggs. It's obvious he knows that there is no nest, no mate, no brood to love. But it is just as obvious that he deeply yearns for it. And it's touching and telling that the only time he opens his fiercely defended phantom nest is to welcome a goose family – Graebel's.

Graebel and his life mates, Ginger and Marianne, are the only living beings who are allowed in Goosifer's yard. Those who don't know Goosifer might assume that he lets the Graebels use his pool because he respects Graebel's unchallenged authority. But the rest of us have learned the hard way that Goosifer respects no one's authority - and we have the welts to prove it. Maybe he lets the Graebels wade and splash in his kiddy pool because he has a crush on Ginger and Marianne and hopes that his gift will win their affection. But Goosifer makes no attempt to connect with them, or even get their attention. He just stands by the pool silently, motionlessly, feet planted on dry ground, and watches Graebel and his mates enjoy the pool together. It could be that watching this goose family passionately engaged in the duties, pleasures and burdens of their life together may be as close as Goosifer will ever get to experiencing it himself. What is certain is that the deep, intimate life union that connects Graebel, Ginger and Marianne is essential to a goose's nature. It's also certain that Goosifer needs it and yearns for it. It is unlikely he will ever know it. But he faithfully reserves a space for it anyway. Goosifer is more or less ignored by other sanctuary residents. But he is emphatically noticed and remembered by most human visitors. Although what we see is probably not Goosifer, as much as our own reflection. We see ourselves in his fears, his comical compulsions, his irrational attachments, his bravado, his vulnerability, his struggle to whittle down the complexity of the world to something manageable: ONE home, ONE loyalty, ONE purpose, ONE love. We also see ourselves in his thwarted nature – his forgotten gooseness reminds us of our own forgotten humanity. When we go through life with our most basic instincts of compassion stifled to the point where we can enjoy the flesh of persons like Goosifer, it's hard to claim that we remember how to be human.

When we know – but choose to forget – that the soul, the face, the mind that was once attached to the piece of meat on our plate was like us in every morally relevant way; when we know – but choose to forget – that the bird we crushed for our soup was a fellow mortal, a flawed, frightened, mysterious being like you and me, who loved life and clung to it as desperately as you and I do, it's hard to claim that there is much left of our humanity.

But, when we refuse to see other animals as anything less than the complex persons they are, when we refuse to consume their flesh, their children, their eggs, their milk, their purpose, we start to reclaim our own purpose, our own forgotten nature; we do what Goosifer does: we reserve a nest, an inviolate space where our most basic instincts of compassion, that are central to our our human nature, can be nurtured and restored.

— *Joanna Lucas*

Barnaby

Aunt Bea

Clover

Chrissie

Warren

Daisy

Farrah & Damien

THE GIFT OF THEIR PRESENCE

In the middle of the night, in their large, multi-tiered enclosure, Farrah and Damien rearrange everything their caretaker has so carefully set out for them. They move food and water dishes to other locations, relocate their litter box, take toys to different shelves. In the morning, if they believe they are not being let out early enough, they bang their toys against the walls of the enclosure. If that doesn't bring results, they do the ultimate rearrangement of their belongings by pushing everything off the shelves into a heap at the bottom.

Farrah and Damien are high-spirited rabbits, two of a litter of seven who, with their mother, were being sold for food in front of a market. A compassionate (and horrified) person bought all of them and took them to a rabbit rescue organization. Jessica – a kind soul who didn't know a lot about "house rabbits" but was eager to learn – adopted Farrah and Damien; the other rabbits in the litter and their mother were adopted by other local families.

These rabbits now spend their days with free run of the house. Rabbits are easily litter box trained and keep themselves meticulously clean, washing themselves like cats. The house has been "rabbit-proofed" for their protection – as rabbits are notorious for chewing on wires and cords, Jessica blocks them from such access with a series of baby gates. Farrah and Damien have been provided with a world of things to do: they have a full wardrobe of toys, which they throw in the air with wild abandon; they have apple and willow branches to chew on, since rabbits need to gnaw to keep their teeth trimmed; and they have places to hide and explore. Damien's favorite hideout is a box behind the recliner, outfitted with a phone book, from which he tears a single page at a time. The "ziiiiip… ziiiiip… ziiiip…" sound of tearing paper confuses visitors to the house until they're told about Damien's meditative hobby.

Rabbits are known to be very curious, and given half a chance, these two hop onto a chair and then onto the dining room table to sniff and explore. They know this is naughty, so when Jessica comes into the room and "catches" them, they do the classic Bugs Bunny move, their back legs running in place but getting no traction on the slick surface of the table. They'll also jump up onto the end table next to the couch, where again, getting no traction, they careen across the table and shoot onto the couch, clearing pictures and water glasses and everything else in their path. They throw the pillows off the couch for fun.

These bunnies know the sound of the refrigerator opening, and will follow you if they know you have raisins. Although Damien pretends to be the boss, he lets Farrah get away with everything, including taking food right out of his mouth.

Rabbits are much more expressive than you'd think. Jessica says if you pay attention and spend the time to get to know them – really know them – you will see that they have facial expressions, and you can tell their mood by their body language: a slight tilt of the ears, the position of the body, how wide open their eyes are.

And if you're not paying attention to those subtle clues, they will let you know of their moods in more overt ways. They seem to have a need to be in charge of little things, and if that need is being subverted, they may turn their backs and flick their back feet at you – a big insult in the rabbit world. Not at all timid, they'll attempt to push you out of the way if you're in their path. They have clear opinions that they're more than willing to share. When Jessica took in another rabbit as a temporary foster guest, Farrah and Damien were not pleased at the intrusion and thumped their feet in disapproval outside the room where the guest was staying.

When they're delighted, they do a move all rabbit guardians know and love: the "binky," in which they throw their bodies in the air and shimmy and twist in joy. This maneuver is tricky and the landings are sometimes miscalculated, sending the bunnies wildly "binkying" into a wall or furniture.

Rabbits are also more affectionate than you'd think. They want to be near their human companions – not so much to be touched and cuddled, but simply not to be alone. If they're blocked from you by a baby gate, they'll stare through it at you, willing you to open it so they may pass. If that doesn't work, they grab the gate with their front teeth and shake it. "All animals want company," says Jessica. "I wouldn't want to be alone either." They do enjoy a certain amount of petting and chatter their teeth – making a sound very much like a cat purring – when the petting is just right.

Rabbits are used by humans in an astonishing variety of ways. In addition to being raised as food, as was intended for Farrah and Damien, they are subjects of painful laboratory experimentation and product testing. They are sold as "pets," then often languish in backyard hutches (suffering from neglect, predators and the extremes of weather) more frequently than being included as members of families. They are raised and killed for their fur, and they are hunted in the wild. Watching Farrah and Damien, it is heartbreaking to imagine these sweet, funny, life-filled creatures being used in any of those ways.

—◇◆◇—

It requires careful thought and a bit of work to provide for rabbits in a way that meets their needs and gives them a happy life. An adopter of two of Farrah and Damien's littermates says, though, that the extra thought and work is more than worth it, simply "for the gift of their presence."

— *Diane Leigh*

Sanctuary

A Day in Their Lives

I awoke before dawn expecting to hear roosters and the general morning hubbub of life on an animal sanctuary, but there was only stillness to my ears and eyes. Michele, the sanctuary's co-founder, knew better; she had seen the mother coyote out hunting and kept her avian friends tucked up safely in their barns. There was no sunrise, just a chilly, wet, gray day that meant everyone's beds — both straw and cotton — were a tad more appealing than early-spring frolicking, so no one was out.

I approached the main barns as breakfast was served. Llamas, goats and cows munched alfalfa together, getting ready for their day. After breakfast, the llamas dispersed into the pastures, with Sampson, as always, standing guard over the herd. They moved slowly and gracefully over the rolling fields.

The goat herd, filled with so many personalities, took quick trips around the pastures as a pack, always circling back up to the main yard to keep tabs on everyone. Shyer goats sometimes hung back in the barns, but most followed Lucy — the leader of the goats, as I learned — in her perambulations. Goats bond in pairs, but the bonds are rooted in companionship, and the pairs can be mates, siblings, same-sex, or older and younger goats. We could learn a lot from their instincts for loyalty and friendship. When one of a bonded pair dies, the living goat does not bond again, instead remaining solitary (though still part of the herd).

Willie was relatively new to the goat herd, having arrived a few months before, and chose the elderly Jeffrey Thomas as his friend. When I visited, Jeffrey Thomas' health was failing and Willie wandered around anxiously, like a relative wringing his hands at the hospital. He followed Michele, seeking reassurances and comfort, and cried plaintively at the fence if he could not follow her. At night, Willie would join Jeffrey Thomas in his barn, trying to wedge his body against Jeffrey's aging one in order to keep him upright and comfortable.

I met other friends in the barn. JC, a grey African goose, is friend to both Sven and Goosifer, two white geese. Sven lurks by the cars, defending from perceived intruders the south side of the house which he was able to claim for himself (in his former life, he had been kept in a chain link dog kennel and was tormented daily by children, with no way to escape the attacks); Goosifer patrols his trash can, pool and wheelbarrow. JC goes back and forth between them, keeping each company. Occasionally, JC leads Goosifer outside the confines of his yard, where they get up to mischief.

There is quite a bit of mischief at the sanctuary. Bumper is a young, rust-colored steer who likes to sneak up on people and, well, bump them, like a rowdy teenager. He is surprisingly stealthy for someone so large. Lucas is a black pig who came to the sanctuary as a piglet after being found running the streets of Denver, having most likely escaped his fate at a slaughterhouse or the transfer to a "fattening paddock." Instead, Lucas found a family, one that both adored and endured him. He was a rambunctious and precocious youngster, tormenting the other residents, but when tempers were tested, all he had to do was let loose with a cry baby squeal and Justice, his bovine protector, would arrive.

Justice, without a doubt, carries an almost preternatural nobility and serenity about him and easily earns the respect given to him by humans and animals alike. He took young Lucas under his wing (so to speak) and allowed the young pig to hide in his shadow when he got into trouble. One day, when the barns were being painted, Lucas tipped over a bucket of paint… and rolled in the paint… and then started chasing the volunteers around like a 700-pound paintbrush. Lucas obviously needed a protector given his personality. Now, as an adult pig he is still very active and has his snout into all manner of affairs.

I learned about the barnyard's other main mischief-maker the hard way. I was in the main chicken yard, photographing the brave, beautiful ladies who were once thought of as nothing more than a source of eggs. I noticed Lerr, a large Leghorn rooster, who hopped up onto the fence and put on quite a show for me, crowing and masculinely posturing. I went back to photographing and watching the hens… until I felt what can only be described as a karate chop to the shin. Lerr was on the ground and wanted me out of his yard. Now! There was no reasoning with the wild gleam in his eye, and after a brief standoff – with me on one leg, trying to protect the other shin, and Lerr on one leg ready to strike again – I quickly backed out of the yard and vacated his dominion.

I decided to wait to return until later, when either the coast was clear or Roy, a large black rooster, was willing to defend me. Michele had told me that Lerr's karate exhibitions were commonplace but that Roy frequently put Lerr in his place, protecting Michele, volunteers and the hens from Lerr's outbursts. The rest of the roosters live in harmony, but Lerr has a bit of a chip on his wing.

It was time to turn my attention to exploring the pastures. There is no such thing as being an impartial observer at the sanctuary. You are pulled into various cliques, nudged, chided, informed, kissed, followed and led. As I walked around the pastures and barns, new animals joined me, as others dropped off the tour. The pack was often comprised of elderly Bluto (a blind dog), hyper Persephone (a young cat), cherubic Beetle Bailey (a potbellied pig), sweet Willie (the anxious goat) and adorable Lotus (a miniature goat). Their running commentary, as well as the distant sounds of the meadowlarks, geese honking, chickens gossiping and bickering, and goats bleating gives the sanctuary its own soundtrack.

The llamas grazed at the perimeters of the land. The open spaces of the prairie at first seemed too empty to my East Coast eyes, but I quickly noticed all the tiny burrows, larger warrens and even bird nests on the ground. I found Justice relaxing with Juliette, Bumper and Laurel. Juliette is a cow who recently became part of the family, and she is very much smitten with Justice. She eats with him, nuzzles him and kisses his shoulders. Laurel, a white swan, is another founding member of Justice's fan club. Laurel's foot is crippled and she moves slowly, but will hobble out to the fields to spend time with Justice, then follow him back into the barn. They move about the sanctuary together with slow and gentle grace. That afternoon, I didn't see the look I had already come to know in Bumper's eye, and knew that I would not be knocked over for amusement… at least not until his siesta was over.

Back at the chicken yard, Lerr was still standing guard at the fence, but I stopped to watch the chickens, turkeys and ducks for a while. I have learned a great deal about birds while photographing for this book. From an early age, I saw chickens, turkeys and other birds as individual beings who could feel pain as I did and so chose not to cause them harm. However, spending months watching so many birds through my viewfinder, I learned so much more about their personalities, endurance and spirit. Birds are not afraid to show you exactly who they are. The vanity of a rooster, the powerful strength of a small hen, the strutting walk of a turkey, the supplication for comfort, the offering of friendship, the flare of defiance, and even joy, naughtiness and worry – it is all there in a look or posture. Often, the hens I have met have suffered greatly, their bodies crippled and beaks maimed, but they are so brave and show such fortitude and resilience. Every rescued hen deserves her own Lifetime movie of the week. Duffy, a white duck, had trouble joining any of the duck groups and instead joined the chicken flock. She bonded with one of the roosters and now spends most of her time acting like one of them. There are also three turkeys in the yard, each with his own personality – gentle Walter, shy Ian and outgoing Clarence. When two baby white ducks arrived, the rest of the birds had no interest, but Fred and Wilma, two African geese, stepped forward to raise Stanley and Hardy. They now travel the sanctuary as a family. Watching all these birds circumnavigate the yard, I am constantly reassessing what I thought I knew, the camera distilling the lessons for me.

Later, cleaning out the barns required a lot of supervision and assistance from the goats, sheep and pigs. It was not unlike attempting to clean litter-boxes at home, only much larger and with a lot more help. Lerr hopped back over the fence to scrutinize my work and flex his feathered biceps in my direction. Satisfied I was under control, he went off to keep an eye on the sheep.

As dinner time rolled around, the residents began to make their way up to the barns. Fresh grain and hay had everyone hopping around. I learned that Lucas, despite his size and tomfoolery, is actually afraid of wee Beetle Bailey, the sweet pot-bellied pig.

This time of day also gave me a chance to meet more of the shyer, quieter residents who, like those in a big family, take a while to meet when there is a gathering. Marty, a goat, peeked at me from one of the barn doors. His ears were severely and painfully docked when he was a baby. I also met Bijou, a sheep, who has nerve damage from being ear-tagged as a baby and cannot raise his head normally. Barney was one of a group of pigs left to die on an abandoned farm in New York state; he and his nine sisters came to live at the sanctuary. The only other male pig at the sanctuary, he is the counterpoint to Lucas's personality, very mellow and soft-spoken. Sylvia, an angora goat, looked like an aging movie star, still photogenic, but wanting the public to leave her alone.

Just outside the main gate are a mother fox and her kits living in a burrow. Despite the propaganda of farming groups, these predators can coexist a matter of feet away from their prey. The mother needs to feed her large brood, Michele acknowledges, so she is cautious to make sure the sanctuary birds are protected and accounted for at dusk. There is only one problem – birds don't like to go to bed early! With the rain, the day should have come to a close early, but birds know when sunset happens and aren't to be cheated out of one of their favorite times of the day. Every time Michele managed to get a few members of the flock put to bed and went to find more, the first group would slip back outside. Meanwhile, the llamas started coming in for the night on their own. Misha seemed to know exactly how to pose like a supermodel on the compost in the deepening twilight; had there been an actual sunset, he would have been twice as breathtaking. Ernestine, one of the pigs, also played on the compost pile a bit and then politely asked me to let her into the pig barn; unlike the birds, she was ready for bedtime. Eventually, one by one, everyone was tucked into bed or made his or her own way there for the night.

There is a simple joy that even the dreariest weather cannot repress at the sanctuary. So many of the animals arrived there after having endured such suffering – you can read it on their faces. But the strength and will to find joy is present as well. There is bliss in a back-scratch or ear-rub. There is delight in fresh hay and practical jokes. In friends and in curiosity. And, most of all, in finding peace and safety. Those who have darker memories of their lives before know the daily joy to be found at the sanctuary.

— *Davida Gypsy Breier*

Farmed Fish and "Seafood"

Aquaculture is the farming of marine and freshwater animals and plants. This includes many species of fish, such as trout, salmon and catfish, as well as shellfish. A report by the Humane Society of the United States claims, "In the United States, 1.3 billion fish are raised in off-shore and land-based aquaculture systems each year for food, making them the second-most commonly farmed animals domestically, following broiler chickens." An estimated 85% of all trout consumed in the United States is farmed, and 30% of all aquatic animals consumed are from the aquaculture industry.

Far from being dim-witted and unfeeling, fish are in fact fascinating, intelligent animals. Zoologist Dr. Theresa Burt de Perera from Oxford University is quoted in the Daily Telegraph as saying, "The public perception of them is that they are pea-brained numbskulls that can't remember things for more than a few seconds. We're now finding that they are very capable of learning and remembering, and possess a range of cognitive skills that would surprise many people." Writing in *Fish and Fisheries,* biologists from the universities of Edinburgh, St. Andrews and Leeds, said that, "Although it may seem extraordinary to those comfortably used to pre-judging animal intelligence on the basis of brain volume, in some cognitive domains, fishes can even be favorably compared to non-human primates."

＞＋＜

Fish "farms" are analogous to any intensely crowded factory farm on land. They could easily be described as underwater factory farms. Like its terrestrial counterpart, the business of aquaculture is to maximize production as much as possible in order to make the most profit. To meet this goal, fish are forced to live in extremely cramped enclosures – usually in pools, concrete tanks or nets – essentially cages of one kind or another. Each is packed with thousands of fish who are unable to swim without continuously careening into each other. A 2002 article in the *Los Angeles Times* stated: "Today, [aquaculture] farms typically put 50,000 to 90,000 fish in a pen 100 feet by 100 feet. A single farm can grow 400,000 fish. Others raise a million or more." This overcrowding causes injuries, stress and death. Many suffer from parasitic infections and various diseases.

When they reach market size, the fish are typically netted then transported to a slaughter facility where they are killed and packaged.

Fish are slaughtered by a variety of methods, all while fully conscious. They may bleed to death after their gills are cut; they may be bludgeoned to death by having their heads crushed; or they may suffocate when the water they are in is drained away. Each of these methods, as you can easily imagine, would be terrifying and painful.

It's a common misconception that fish don't feel pain. Because they are not mammals – like we are – and like cows and pigs are – they seem very different from us, and it is easy to think that they don't experience the world in any of the same ways we do, so it is equally easy to dismiss them, their lives, their suffering, and their deaths.

But it is indisputable: fish feel pain. For many years, this concept has been questioned and debated but today there is no doubt that fish have complex nervous systems that recognize and respond to pain. Cambridge University scientist Dr. Donald Broom is widely quoted as saying, "The scientific literature is quite clear. Anatomically, physiologically and biologically, the pain system in fish is virtually the same as in birds and mammals." Though they may not make sounds of distress and agony like other animals, fish feel pain with the same nervous system you and I do.

A recent study by scientists at Queen's University in Belfast indicates that crustaceans — such as lobsters, crab and shrimp — also feel pain and stress. No question about it: being boiled alive hurts.

Jean

Even if fish or other aquatic animals are not products of the aquaculture system — meaning, they are "wild caught" — there are good reasons to avoid eating them.

One is the issue of "bycatch" — fish that are too small to take, or are not the target species being caught. It is estimated that 85% of the catch made by shrimp trawlers is "bycatch" consisting of turtles, sharks, birds, fish, seals and other animals, which is thrown back overboard. As many as 40,000 sea turtles are killed this way every year. It could be argued that shrimp is the most environmentally devastating "seafood" one could eat.

Another is the simple reality of over-fishing. The United Nations' Food and Agriculture Organization estimates that 70% of the world's fish species are either fully exploited or their population is depleted to some degree. Boris Worm, the lead author of a report published in the journal *Science* estimates that "if the long-term trend continues, all fish and seafood species are projected to collapse within my lifetime – by 2048."

⇒•◆•⇐

This is just a brief overview of a topic that has not received much public atention. Even just the few statistics above are shocking. For a thorough examination of the issues surrounding this subject, read the report by The Humane Society of the United States entitled "The Welfare of Animals in the Aquaculture Industry." You can find it at www.hsus.org.

— *Marilee Geyer*

Afterword

We hope you've enjoyed reading the stories, seeing the photos of these animals, and learning of their remarkable personalities, depth, and individuality.

It can be surprising to discover how complex they are. That surprise is testament to how deep our culture's training goes – training that wants us to believe that the intelligence and feeling has been bred out of farmed animals, leaving them numb and empty, and that they somehow don't value their own lives in the same way we value ours.

But when we looked into their eyes we didn't see emptiness. When we learned how they live – when they are just left to be who they are – we saw not numbness but full, complicated lives, and a constellation of feelings and emotions.

They're different from us, that much is true, but different doesn't mean lesser. They surely experience the world in ways that we don't. And yet, as the stories in this book have shown, they experience many of the same things that we do: friends, family, others they like, some they don't, some they *love*. Pleasure, fun, joy. The grief of losing someone. Favorite things, things disliked. A difficult past, that some have

Saffron

trouble shaking, haunting them. A hopeful future, that some seem to embrace, headed full-throttle into their new lives.

But let us remember: Justice, comforter of newcomers, was intended to become organic hamburger and steaks. Lucas – sweet Lucas, in love with Petunia – was destined to be bacon. The toddlers Jeremy & Lenny were taken from their mother so she would provide us with goat milk. Libby, protected by her loving Louie, was to live a shortened life in a shed to give us her "free-range" eggs. Amelia would have been a Thanksgiving dinner.

And there's no reason to think that the other 10 billion animals raised each year for their meat, milk and eggs are any less interesting, or any less unique, than the ones in this book. They each could have had a life that they explored and lived and loved. Ten billion a year… individuals, one and all.

———◆———

Most of us would rather not know about the harsh realities of raising animals for food. We've touched on some of those realities in this book, and there are more that we haven't touched on. There is much about how farmed animals are treated to be concerned about, and heartbroken by.

But it goes beyond how they're treated when they're alive. It's that then they are killed, and although we can hope and want to believe that the killing is done "humanely," it's just not possible. There is no way to kill the sheer numbers of animals we do – *billions* each year – and have it be anything less than an assembly line of terror. What must it be like to be loaded into a truck, driven for hours or days, then unloaded and put in line to wait your turn to die, watching ahead as your herd-mates, or your flock-mates, go down that line, disappearing one by one, into the building that smells like death? And it wouldn't matter if it were done in a family farmyard instead – aren't all living beings afraid and suffering when their lives are being forcibly taken from them? As one of the sanctuary caretakers told us, "It can never be humane for the individual. We *all* fight for our lives."

Even the animals raised for their milk and eggs are killed. It's obvious that animals must die for us to have their meat, but egg laying hens also have to die when they're no longer productive enough to be financially profitable. Dairy cows

Agnes & Althea

and goats don't get put out to pasture when they wear out, that wouldn't be financially expedient, so they have to die, too. And the offspring of all them, when not put back into the system, are killed as newborns. *All* farmed animals eventually are killed – and always before their time, nobody gets to grow old – because it's always an economic decision.

The basics of animal agriculture are this: We decide who will be their mothers and fathers. We manipulate their genetics. We artificially inseminate them. We decide how their babies will be born. We decide how long, if at all, the babies will be allowed to stay with their mothers. We decide where they live, how they live, and what they get to do. What they will eat. Who they will live with. How long – how many days, how many months, mostly; sometimes,

how many years – they will live. We decide the day they will die, and how they will die, and then we send them off to that death.

They have their own lives, and their own experiences of relationships, emotions, and feelings… and we take that whole realm of living – of *being* – away from them. We take their lives, in every way, and on every level. Could it ever be right to take Justice from his hills and sky and his friends? Could it ever be right to take Libby away from her Louie? Could it be right to take Amelia from her peaceful enjoyment of her own days? Can it ever be right to take any of them from the lives they own, and the world they see?

We humbly thank you for reading this book, and opening yourself to the animals and their stories. We hope they touched both your mind *and* your heart. And we hope you might picture the other animals, just like the ones you've read about – the ones in sheds, in cages, on tractor trailers – who are not being rescued and taken in by a sanctuary. And, naturally, we hope you will think about what you do in your everyday life, and how it might affect them.

Having looked into their eyes – the "windows of the souls" – and having *found* souls, we know that we are somehow changed. We hope you are too.

– Diane Leigh

Oliver

Eva & Nemo

About the Portraits

The beautiful silhouetted cow opposite the title page and on the back cover is **Bosey**, who was rescued as part of a neglect case in New York. She now lives at Farm Sanctuary's New York Shelter, where she is currently one of the oldest members of the cattle herd.
— *Photo by Derek Goodwin*

More than 300 million layer hens just like **Gilly** (p. 1), **Glynda, Gilda** and **Wilhelmina** (p. 5) live in the United States under deplorable battery cage egg factory conditions.

You'll notice that the hens have deformed beaks. That's because they have been "de-beaked." When jam-packed into battery cages, hens will peck each other out of boredom, frustration, stress and fear. In order to reduce injuries from this unnatural behavior, it's standard industry practice to cut off part of the beak when they are chicks – a procedure done with a hot blade that severs bone, cartilage and soft tissue – all without pain relief. Many chicks die outright from shock. Those who survive live the rest of their lives without a fully functioning beak which they would normally use for exploring their surroundings and picking up food and other objects.

The hens also suffer from osteoporosis because their bodies use more calcium than they get from their diet to form shells for the artificially-high numbers of eggs they lay. An article in *Poultry Science* (vol 83, Issue 2) states, "…evidence suggests that [osteoporosis] may be widespread and severe. If true, most caged laying hens suffer osteoporosis-related bone fracture during the first laying cycle. Osteoporosis also makes bone breakage a serious problem during catching and transport of hens prior to slaughter. Estimates of mortality due to osteoporosis in commercial caged layer flocks are few, but range up to a third of total mortality. Many of these deaths would be lingering and attended by emaciation and possibly pain. …Overall, the evidence indicates that cage layer osteoporosis is a serious animal welfare problem."
— *Gilly & Wilhelmina by Marilee Geyer*
— *Glynda & Gilda by Windi Wojdak*

Rudy (p. 6) was brought to Poplar Spring Sanctuary when he was just a youngster. Pygmy goats are farmed for both meat and milk, and because of their small stature, they are often found in "petting zoos." Rudy doesn't concern himself with any of that, though. He's just who he is: affectionate, adorable, lovable, and playful.
— *Photo by Davida Gypsy Breier*

Peapod (p. 7) is another Poplar Spring resident. He was the "prize" in a greased pig contest. The person who "won" Peapod took him into the parking lot where he began beating and throwing rocks at him; other people joined in. A security guard witnessed this and was able to intervene. Peapod was taken in by a local rescue and then made his way to the sanctuary.
— *Photo by Davida Gypsy Breier*

Rhubarb (p. 8) is a Rhode Island Red rooster who lives at United Poultry Concerns (UPC) in Virginia where he is very protective of the flock. When he spots danger, he lets out a shrill cry that alerts the other hens and roosters. When the threat is gone, he gives an "all clear" crow that lets everyone know all is well.
— *Photo by Davida Gypsy Breier*

Francine (p. 9) is a little brown hen who, because of her very severe debeaking, has some trouble foraging and pecking. But she still manages to enjoy the many treats she receives at her home at UPC. For more information on all types of poultry, or to find out how to visit this "Poultry Paradise," go to www.upc-online.org
— *Photo by Davida Gypsy Breier*

All varieties of domestic chickens are descended from Red Jungle Fowl, a wild bird found in Southeast Asia. **Francine** and her best pal **Iris** (p.9) have an instinctual desire to roost in the branches of trees and bushes, just like their undomesticated relatives and ancestors.
— *Photo by Davida Gypsy Breier*

Benjamin (p. 10) was left one cold day at the bottom of UPC's yard next to the road. He was found alone and shivering in a plastic box with a brick on top. When he met the other residents, all of the chickens – including the other roosters! – welcomed him into their flock. Everybody loves dear, sweet Benjamin.
— *Photo by Davida Gypsy Breier*

Violet (p. 10) was rescued from a major veterinary school battery cage research facility. Large numbers of farmed animals are used in university agricultural research projects, and at some veterinary schools animals are used for "practice" surgeries. Fortunately for Violet, her university days are over; she is free from the battery cage and enjoying her life at Farm Sanctuary in New York.
— *Photo by Derek Goodwin*

Julia, Zenobia and **Jolene,** (p.11) shown here relaxing at UPC, are bred for laying huge numbers of eggs. Although factory farmed hens are never allowed to hatch chicks, hens make excellent mothers and form strong family attachments. A mother hen begins bonding with her babies by clucking to her unhatched chicks, who will chirp back through their shells.
— *Photo by Davida Gypsy Breier*

Elinor (p. 12) is a lovely hen who spends her days with her friend Troubadour, a handsome rooster, in their yard at UPC. They sleep together at night on their enclosed porch.
— *Photo by Davida Gypsy Breier*

Kathleen (p. 12) spent the first 22 months of her life in a cramped cage, producing eggs at a factory farm in Rhode Island. She and 12 of her sisters were rescued and came to live at UPC. Scared and bedraggled at first, Kathleen is flourishing with her new freedoms and family.
— *Photo by Davida Gypsy Breier*

Libby and **Louie** (pgs. 18, 21) spend their days together at Peaceful Prairie Sanctuary in Deer Trail, Colorado. Libby came from a "cage-free" egg factory, a label that some people equate with "humane." Sadly, the public is led to believe that "cage-free" hens live a happy, natural life. This is simply not so. These hens come from the same hatcheries that battery hens come from, all of their brothers are killed, the girls themselves endure the same bodily manipulations and mutilations and they all ultimately end up at the same slaughter-houses when their "production" declines.

Just as dogs, cats and other companion animals are often lost or abandoned, so too are farmed animals. **Goldie** (p.13) was found stray on the streets, but now has safe refuge at the Center for Animal Protection and Education in California. Visit www.capeanimals.org for more information on their life-saving programs.
— *Photo by Windi Wojdak*

Visit www.peacefulprairie.org to read their pamphlet comparing "free-range" eggs and battery eggs and see if you can tell the difference.
— *Photos by Joanna Lucas*

Chickens like **Madeline** (pgs.14, 16) who are raised for their flesh typically live their entire short lives in huge overcrowded windowless sheds that hold as many as 20,000 birds.

In addition to causing great suffering, these conditions lead to unbelievable filth and disease. A report by the Humane Society of the United States on the welfare of animals in the chicken industry found that, "The overwhelming majority of the more than nine billion chickens slaughtered for meat in the United States each year are raised in industrial production systems that severely impair their welfare. These animals experience crowded confinement, unnatural lighting regimes, poor air quality, stressful handling and transportation, and inadequate stunning and slaughter procedures …" The entire report can be found at: www.hsus.org.
— *Photos by Windi Wojdak*

Rootie (p.24), was rescued by a woman who found him, neglected and emaciated, at a friend's neighbor's farmyard. The farmer considered Rootie the runt of the litter and not worth the time and trouble to care for and planned to kill him. The woman intervened and he now enjoys life at the Center for Animal Protection and Education.
— *Photo by Windi Wojdak*

When floods devastated the Midwest, **Krusty's** (p. 25) mother Rosebud swam for her life after evacuees left her behind. In the most ambitious rescue in Farm Sanctuary history, the organization came to the aid of Rosebud and more than 60 other pigs who were stranded in the disaster zone. Shortly after her arrival at their New York Shelter, Rosebud gave birth to Krusty and six other piglets.
— *Photo by Natalie Bowman*

Used as a "teaching tool" at a university veterinary hospital, **Johnny** (p. 25) was treated as a prop, mutilated and nearly sent to slaughter once his "usefulness" had expired. Upon hearing he would be sold at auction, a student pleaded for his life, and because of her courageous stand, Johnny lives happily at Farm Sanctuary's California Shelter.
— *Photo by Connie Pugh*

According to the Woodstock Farm Animal Sanctuary website, **Patsy** (p.26) and her siblings were found in a tiny pen with no shelter. Acting on a tip that horses were being neglected at the site, officers investigated and discovered the scared, hungry motherless piglets, along with two frightened horses. They were all seized and held until placement could be arranged.
— *Photo by Bob Esposito*

Rescued from certain death on a factory hog farm, **Fiona** (p.27) had endured much abuse by the time she came to the sanctuary. At just under two weeks of age she had already been cruelly tail-docked without anesthesia and ripped from her mother's side to be primed for the commercial food chain. Now strong, healthy and free, Fiona lives the good life at Farm Sanctuary's New York Shelter.
— *Photo by Erin Howard*

Joan Jett (p. 27, front) came to Farm Sanctuary's New York Shelter after being rescued during a factory farm cruelty investigation. She was cold, scared and malnourished when she was discovered, but quickly gained strength and self confidence and settled into the gentle pace of sanctuary life. Joan is one of the first pigs to jump up and greet visitors with a jovial grunt, along with her friends **Andy** and **Tim.**
— *Photo by Natalie Bowman*

Maggie and **Aurora** (p.28) were being taken from a factory farm to a slaughterhouse when the driver parked his triple-decker trailer and then abandoned it, leaving the animals in the hot sun without water. The trailer was seized and the pigs were taken to Poplar Spring Sanctuary. Forty of them, including Maggie and Aurora, went to Farm Sanctuary's New York Shelter to live out the rest of their lives.
— *Photo by Derek Goodwin*

Rosie and **Ronnie** (p. 29) were also on the abandoned livestock truck. Although the corporation who owned the pigs was not prosecuted for abandoning them, they agreed to sign the pigs over to Poplar Spring in lieu of paying them $10,000 to cover expenses. Rosie and Ronnie went to Farm Sanctuary in New York, where they lived happily all the rest of their days.
— *Photo by Derek Goodwin*

Lucas (pgs. 30, 33) lives at Peaceful Prairie Sanctuary and no one visits there without being greeted and escorted everywhere by him. Pigs are highly intelligent, curious and social animals who suffer terribly in factory farms where they are denied their most basic needs and desires. They live in what the pork industry calls "concentrated animal feeding operations" where thousands of pigs are crammed into dank windowless buildings with air quality so poor that death and disease are common. Many pigs become crazy with boredom and develop neurotic behaviors such as banging their heads on the metal bars of their pens or biting them compulsively. After enduring much misery in these appalling conditions, the pigs are slaughtered when they reach six months of age.
— *Adult Lucas photo by Davida Gypsy Breier*
— *Baby Lucas photo by Michele Alley-Grubb*

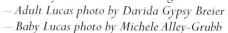

Sophie (p. 34) lives at the Woodstock Farm Animal Sanctuary. Roughly 105 million pigs are raised and slaughtered in the U.S. each year. On factory farms, a mother pig becomes a piglet-making machine and spends her entire life in a gestation crate, an individual metal enclosure so small she can't turn around or even lie down comfortably. Such confinement causes much physical and psychological suffering.
— *Photo by Bob Esposito*

Judy (p. 36) is Patsy's sister. These girls were fortunate to have been rescued, but without farmed animal sanctuaries, farmed animals would have few options. It is common for them to be euthanized after being seized or surrendered because dog and cat shelters often do not have the facilities or resources to care for these animals and adopters can be difficult to find.
— *Photo by Bob Esposito*

Abbey (p. 38) was part of a cruelty case involving 30 starving dairy cows in New York. Here, she strikes a beautiful autumn pose in the pasture of her Farm Sanctuary home.
— *Photo by Derek Goodwin*

Lying alone on the side of a road, **Whitaker** (p. 39) was only days old and hours from death when his rescuers found him — too weak, too sick and too young to stand very well on his own. They scooped him up, took him to a veterinarian for treatment, and after finding Farm Sanctuary online, brought him to their California shelter where he made a full recovery.
— *Photo by Connie Pugh*

Heidi (p. 40) was one of 2,000 calves born to a herd of dairy cows. Most were killed shortly after birth. Heidi was taken by a farmer, but when he sent her to slaughter she refused to enter the trailer. She escaped twice and just when it seemed her luck had run out, a kind person purchased her freedom. She now lives at Poplar Spring Animal Sanctuary.
— *Photo by Davida Gypsy Breier*

Loretta's (p. 40) baby was found near death by a humane officer and confiscated. Later, mother and son were reunited to live at Farm Sanctuary. Such reunions are rare in farm animal rescue work, but having the opportunity to shelter these two from an industry that inevitably tears farm animal families apart is a true gift, unmatched for the animals and for the rescuers.
— *Photo by Connie Pugh*

Born at a dairy, separated from his mother and sent to auction as a newborn, **Eli** (p. 41) was abandoned at a stockyard when he failed to sell for even one dollar. Fortunately, he was rescued along with four other Jersey calves and taken to Farm Sanctuary's California Shelter. Eli lived a long, happy life until he passed away in 2007.
— *Photo by Derek Goodwin*

Separated from his mother soon after his birth at a dairy farm that had no use for him because he would never produce milk, **Casey** (p. 42) was cast aside by workers and wound up in the back of a slaughterhouse-bound truck. Fortunately, he was rescued by a Farm Sanctuary investigator and found his way to the organization's California Shelter, where he lives a full happy life.
— *Photo by Connie Pugh*

Harrison (p. 43) is Loretta's baby. A humane officer found him near death and rushed him to a veterinarian to be treated for a severe infection. Loretta was also rescued and after convalescing, a healthier and happier mother-son duo traveled to Farm Sanctuary's California Shelter, where they remain inseparable – living each day as if there was never any reality different from the one they now know.
— *Photo by Connie Pugh*

Herbie (p. 44), a four month old Hereford calf, led police through the streets of Brooklyn after he jumped from a truck taking him to slaughter. After he was caught, Herbie was taken to an animal control facility. After a mandatory holding period, a minivan from the Woodstock Farm Animal Sanctuary arrived to take Herbie to safety.
— *Photo by Bob Esposito*

Juliette (p. 44) and her son escaped from a family farm and headed for Peaceful Prairie Sanctuary. To get there, she broke through several fences and ran a great distance trying to lead her son to safety. Sadly, the farmer demanded the calf be returned and though Juliette was safe, she suffered the greatest tragedy any mother could experience: the loss of her precious child.
— *Photo by Davida Gypsy Breier*

A pregnant Misty was one of 26 cattle rescued by Farm Sanctuary. She was used as a "breeding cow" forced to give birth so that her calves could be used for veal or beef. When their babies are torn from them, cows cry for days. Fortunately, Misty will never experience such a loss again. She and her son **David** (p. 45) now live happily together with a family in Michigan.
— *Photo by Derek Goodwin*

Ralphie (p. 46) along with **Andy** and **Elvis** (p. 47) live at Woodstock Farm Animal Sanctuary, whose website explains: "Many people do not realize that veal is a direct by-product of the dairy industry. To maximize milk production, farmers artificially inseminate cows every year. Female offspring are kept to make future milking cows.

Male calves are taken from their mothers shortly after birth. In the U.S. most are destined for veal crates where they will endure 14 to 17 weeks of torture in a pen so small they can't even turn around. With dairy cows it is not economically viable to raise the males for beef. Their flesh is not as desirable as the 'beef' breeds … so they become veal instead."
— *Photos by Bob Esposito*

Had he not been rescued, **Charley** (pgs. 48, 51), who was likely born on a relatively small farm, would have been sent to the local auction. After sale, he would have been transported to an order buyer's barn then sold again to a feedlot.

In these vast, barren lots as many as 50,000 animals are crowded into filthy pens with no shelter from the elements. Overcrowding and an unnatural diet meant to induce rapid weight gain contribute to a myriad of health and welfare problems. Standing day in and day out in mud, snow and manure, young steers spend several months here before finally being loaded and shipped to a slaughter plant for a frightening end to a miserable life.
— *Photos by Windi Wojdak*

Justice (pgs. 52–55) was very lucky to have survived his escape from the slaughter truck and find refuge at Peaceful Prairie Sanctuary.

Cattle may travel hundreds or even thousands of miles to slaughter on a journey that may take days. These long journeys, without food and only infrequent water, are very stressful and many animals die along the way. They are exposed to the extremes of weather; in the summer they may collapse from the heat, and in the cold winter months some actually freeze to the sides of the truck.

When they arrive at the slaughterhouse, they are shot in the head with a captive bolt pistol, shackled, hung by their legs then moved to the killing floor where their throats are cut and they are skinned and dismembered.

Because the captive bolt procedure is imperfect, some animals are not rendered unconscious, but instead are fully awake and aware, kicking, struggling and bellowing, throughout the entire ordeal. Their suffering is unimaginable.
— *Photos by Windi Wojdak*

During birth, **Linda** (p. 56) was pulled incorrectly from her mother's womb and Linda's pelvis was crushed. Considering her "damaged goods," the farmer did not want her; she likely would have been "discarded" or sold to slaughter, but a kind man intervened and called Farm Sanctuary. Although she will always have issues with her back legs, sanctuary life is perfect for this charismatic, friendly girl.
— *Photo by Lesley Marino*

Strong friendships, like **Tricia** (p. 58) and Linda's at Farm Sanctuary in New York are not unusual. In fact, cattle, just like humans, form special bonds with one another and will spend most of their time together, frequently grooming and licking each other. Cattle also experience strong emotions from joy and love to loneliness and fear.
— *Photo by Erin Howard*

Rochester (p. 60) was rescued by Farm Sanctuary from a man who was raising turkeys in his basement for the Thanksgiving market. Each year, 46 million turkeys are slaughtered for Thanksgiving meals.
— *Photo by Derek Goodwin*

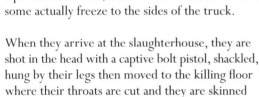

Sammy (pg. 61) lives at Woodstock Farm Animal Sanctuary in New York. Approximately 300 million turkeys are slaughtered every year in this country and although the Humane Methods of Slaughter Act requires animals be stunned or otherwise rendered insensible prior to shackling and slaughter, this law does not apply to turkeys, chickens or other poultry.
— *Photo by Bob Esposito*

Helen (p. 62) was rescued from an animal shelter where she had been brought in as a stray. She now lives at the Center for Animal Protection and Education and delights friends and visitors with her charming array of melodious coos, murmurs, chirps and other sounds of sweet turkey music.
— *Photo by Windi Wojdak*

Hannah (p. 62) and three other young turkeys were found abandoned in a cardboard box, without food or water, at a shopping center. They were dehydrated and in desperate need of nourishment. After a kind couple found and rescued them, Hannah and the others found their way to Farm Sanctuary's California Shelter, where they enjoy serene, contented lives.
— *Photo by Connie Pugh*

Boone, Herschel and **Alphonso** (p. 63) arrived at Woodstock Farm Animal Sanctuary and quickly became known as "The Committee." Always found together and always found in discussion, "The Committee" strutted about the farm v-e-r-y s-l-o-w-l-y. Yet, no matter how fast one hurried about the farm, "The Committee" seemed always to be just five feet behind you. Always uncanny and always endearing.
— *Photo by Bob Esposito*

Aubrey (p. 64) came to live at United Poultry Concerns when he was a young bird. He is still young, but his legs can no longer support his weight. Each morning he is carried out of his barn and placed in the center of the yard to enjoy the sunlight, being sprinkled with the hose, and the company of volunteers and other birds.
— *Photo by Davida Gypsy Breier*

Jewle (p. 65) was on the same airplane as Rhoslyn and Ariala (next page) where 13,000 baby turkeys died from overcrowding, asphyxiation, overheating and dehydration. While 1,900 of the survivors were sent to their final destination to become "breeders" whose offspring would be sold for food, Jewle was one of 11 baby turkeys rescued and given refuge at Farm Sanctuary's California Shelter.
— *Photo by Connie Pugh*

Melvin (pgs. 66–69) and his brothers arrived at Peaceful Prairie Sanctuary when they were only four months old. They had been painfully de-beaked and de-toed, had never seen the light of day, been forced to live in filthy overcrowded conditions and would have been trucked to slaughter if it weren't for the fact that they were the apparent victims of a high school prank: students broke into a school and left the six petrified turkeys in the cafeteria.

All six recovered from their ordeal and were rescued by Peaceful Prairie so they could live out their lives unmolested and free to enjoy the pleasures of life.

Turkeys are extremely social, curious and intelligent birds. When they aren't crammed in factory or so-called "free-range" farms, they spend their time doing what turkeys like and want to do: they care for their babies, forage for food, play, squabble, form relationships, live their lives.
—*Melvin's portrait by Joanna Lucas*
—*Melvin and his brothers and Melvin and Ruth by Michele Alley-Grubb*

Modern turkeys like **Amelia** (pgs. 70–71) are bred to grow as large as possible as quickly as possible. They are hatched in incubators and never have the chance to see or learn from their mothers. Like chickens raised for their flesh, turkeys spend their entire lives in large windowless buildings. They are forced to live in feces, and the ammonia fumes are so strong that it burns their eyes and lungs. Millions of them die

during the first few weeks of life.

In his book *The Food Revolution,* John Robbins cites the following from industry publication *Lancaster Farming:* "If a seven pound human baby grew at the same rate, the infant would weigh 1,500 pounds at just 18 weeks of age."
— *Photos by Davida Gypsy Breier*

Rhoslyn (p. 72) and **Ariala** (p. 74; both p. 73) recuperated from their airplane ordeal and were later adopted into a loving home. Farm Sanctuary's website has this additional information: "The bird-shipping industry has a poor track record of ensuring animal welfare. It ships millions of birds across the country via postal mail and as cargo aboard airlines, and countless numbers perish from heat extremes, overcrowding and deprivation of food and water ...."

"Sadly, if these birds had not suffered the way they did at the hands of careless cargo workers, they would surely have been sent to work as 'breeders' within an industry that only regards them as a means to produce more turkeys for cold-cuts and holiday meals. To meet consumer demand for breast meat, commercial turkeys have been bred to have abnormally large breasts. As a result, the birds cannot mount and reproduce naturally, and the industry now relies on artificial insemination as the sole means of reproduction. The 1,900 turkeys that survived ... will endure a constant cycle of forced 'milking' of the toms and artificial insemination of the hens, until their bodies give out and they are sent to slaughter."
— *Photos by Windi Wojdak*

Annie (p. 76) was discovered at a California slaughterhouse with nearly 70 other animals, ill and malnourished enough to cause a humane officer to open an investigation. More than a dozen goats and a cow were seized and given refuge at Farm Sanctuary's California Shelter.
— *Photo by Connie Pugh*

Molly (p. 77) and her daughter Morgan were rescued together from a farm where dogs continually broke in and attacked the animals who lived there. They remain together to this day at Farm Sanctuary's California Shelter, and despite the fact that Molly's ripped ear bears the permanent scar of the attacks, if you met the goats today, you'd never know they had had such a rough beginning.
— *Photo by Connie Pugh*

Jordan (p. 77) was rescued by Farm Sanctuary from the Lancaster, Pennsylvania stockyards. He was a "downer" suffering from salt toxicity/water deprivation. "Downer" is the term the meat and dairy industries use to refer to animals so sick, diseased or disabled that they cannot even stand on their own. Jordan lived 15 long, happy years at their New York Shelter before he passed away several years ago.
— *Photo by Derek Goodwin*

Swoozie (p. 78) was rescued with Annie. Despite the condition of the animals, the California Department of Agriculture determined that they posed no health risk to consumers — essentially allowing for the continued operation of the facility and the prolonged suffering of the animals who remained there, simply because they hadn't yet fallen to such extreme neglect that they could legally be removed by animal control.
— *Photo by Connie Pugh*

Simon (p. 78) was a seven-pound baby pygmy goat when he was found wandering the streets of Brooklyn. He was underweight, cold, alone, scared, and suffering from severe pneumonia, lice infestation, sore mouth and giardiasis when a caring woman found him. Eventually, he came to Farm Sanctuary's New York Shelter. After receiving medical treatment and lots of love, he fully recovered.
— *Photo by Derek Goodwin*

Paloma (p. 79) was about to be sent to slaughter from a dairy operation when she was rescued by a volunteer from BrightHaven, a nonprofit holistic animal retreat dedicated to the well-being of senior, disabled and special needs animals. Their sole and uncompromising vision is to help many animals live out long lives in peace and happiness. To learn more, visit www.BrightHaven.org
— *Photo by Marilee Geyer*

Tanya and **Raposal** (p. 80) and **Hal** (p. 80) were rescued with Annie and Swoozie from the California slaughterhouse. Emaciated, injured and critically ill when they were discovered, all four had been so severely neglected that the humane officer who found and seized them feared for their lives. The officer learned that the animals had either been bred on the property or acquired at auction by the slaughterhouse owner and confined in the feedlot, until local customers hand-select them for slaughter on site – much like the live animal markets in urban centers such as New York City. The sickest animals had likely been on the property the longest and therefore had come closest to succumbing before even reaching the kill floor.
— *Photos by Connie Pugh*

Cheech (p. 81) was abandoned at a farm and was about to be sent to a livestock auction where he would have been sold for slaughter. Fortunately, Farm Sanctuary heard about his fate and convinced authorities to release him; he has been enjoying his life at their California Shelter ever since. Photographer Connie Pugh says that although his old body is aging, his spirit remains young and strong.
— *Photo by Connie Pugh*

Olivia (p. 82, 85; p. 84 with **Albie**) found love and safety at Woodstock Farm Animal Sanctuary. Her profile at www.WoodstockSanctuary.org states, "Olivia spent an estimated three months living in the backyard of the abandoned home. Olivia's water source became whatever puddles resulted from rain, and without proper care, Olivia became infested with internal parasites causing her to lose weight. The worst part was her hoof neglect. Domesticated goats must have their hooves trimmed because unlike wild goats, they're not jumping around on mountains and rocks and keeping them worn down. Olivia's hooves grew out like Turkish slippers, and this caused the ligaments in her legs to deform making it difficult to walk.

When Olivia was finally rescued by humane law and brought to the sanctuary, she was treated like a queen .... She became one of the most memorable animals on the farm because of her fantasy-like beauty and her tendency to get playfully feisty. She knew how to impress visitors."

Photographer Bob Esposito adds that Olivia was a natural character when it came to the camera and that she was adored by all who met her.
— *Photos by Bob Esposito*

Jeremy and **Lenny** (p. 86; Jeremy, p. 87; Lenny, p. 88) were very fortunate to have been rescued and brought to Poplar Spring Sanctuary. Often, the male offspring of dairy goats are sent to auction. Compassion Over Killing conducted an investigation of livestock auctions and found that violence and intimidation toward animals are the norm. "Farmed animals are brought to livestock auctions to be sold to the highest bidder, from small farmers to factory farms to slaughter companies. To the sellers and buyers, the only worth of these animals lies in the economic value of their flesh, milk, wool, and other marketable qualities.

At auctions, animals have no control over their fate. Confused and terrified, they are kicked and prodded, separated from their companions, forced into the auction ring, bid on, and then trucked off, now the property of a new owner. Unable to understand the new and foreign environment, animals at auctions routinely become immobilized in the chutes. For those who can't free themselves, workers shock them with electric prods and beat them. Animals who are either unable or unwilling to walk are dragged by their legs, ears, and tails by workers …." Read the full report at www.cok.net.
—*Photos by Davida Gypsy Breier*

Ray-Ray (p. 90) is in fact a she who lives at the Woodstock Farm Animal Sanctuary. Domesticated sheep have been bred to grow more wool than they would naturally need which often leads to skin sores, fly infestations and parasites. Rough handling is common during shearing and many of the panicky sheep are cut or otherwise injured during the process.
— *Photo by Bob Esposito*

Georgie (p. 91) has a safe home at Peaceful Prairie Sanctuary, but growing demand for meat from ritually slaughtered animals has led to an increase in the number of sheep and goats marketed for that purpose. Ritual slaughter laws require that animals be fully conscious while their throats are cut and the blood drained from their bodies. Often they are shackled and hung by a back leg while killed.
— *Photo by Windi Wojdak*

Disoriented, lost, terrified and very pregnant, **Wendy** (p. 91, back) was a lone sheep on the loose until she found herself stuck in a roadside ditch full of water and mud, completely unable to move. After being rescued by local animal control, Wendy was given refuge at Farm Sanctuary's California Shelter, where she gave birth to **Ady** and **Colvin** just days after her arrival.
— *Photo by Connie Pugh*

This beautiful face belongs to **Doris** (p. 92) who lives at Peaceful Prairie Sanctuary. Painful tail docking is performed on most sheep in this country. The most common method is to apply a rubber ring around the tail of a days-old lamb. The ring cuts off the blood supply, the tail "dies" and in seven to ten days falls off, or is sometimes cut off before that point.
— *Photo by Windi Wojdak*

Devlin (p. 92) arrived at the Woodstock Farm Animal Sanctuary with a sad story but a happy ending. Rescued from an overcrowded farm, he was found in a basement brimming with feces, and without food or water. Devlin has put the past behind him and now bravely runs up to newcomers and leans into their legs waiting to be scratched deep into his wool.
— *Photo by Bob Esposito*

Ewegenia (p. 93) was abandoned with another ewe, Ewedora and a ram, Rambam, after the tenants on the property on which they lived moved. The owner of the property cared for them only sporadically and when they began to starve, a concerned neighbor convinced the owner to surrender the sheep to animal control. They were adopted by a family who cherish and adore them.
— *Photo by Windi Wojdak*

Daisy, Adam, Dorothy, and **Hickory** (p. 94), affectionately dubbed "The Professors" because of their scholarly gazes, live at Poplar Spring Sanctuary. Although often portrayed as "simple" animals, sheep are interesting, complex, unique, emotional individuals, with highly developed social awareness and interactions - just like human beings.
— *Photo by Davida Gypsy Breier*

Ashton (p. 95) is a personality-beaming, charismatic, woolly force. Arriving at Woodstock Farm Animal Sanctuary as a scrawny lamb with mouth infections, Ashton's outgoing but friendly ways soon slotted him in as one of the top sheep of his barn. Ashton is a true charmer.
— *Photo by Bob Esposito*

Lucky Lady (pgs. 96–97) cheated death by escaping from an auction house and roaming the streets of New York City for hours. The 65-pound lamb was eventually caught by police and taken to Animal Care & Control. Farm Sanctuary was contacted and they agreed to take in the months-old lamb. She arrived at their bucolic New York Shelter a few days later; a far cry from the bustling city and its many slaughterhouses.

Lucky Lady recovered from her ordeal and will spend the rest of her days enjoying a spacious pasture, warm barn and the company of friends.
— *Lucky Lady's portrait by Susie Coston*
— *Lucky Lady and friends by Derek Goodwin*

Sheep like **Marcie** (pgs. 98–100) are used by the animal agriculture industry for their meat, wool, milk and skin. Even though most sheep live outside, the idea that they lead a pleasant life in grassy fields is a myth, as they too suffer from an economic system that tries to derive as much product as possible from an animal before he or she is killed.

Normally, sheep breed once a year and have one or two lambs. The ewe becomes fertile in the fall or winter and the lambs are born in the warmer months. Modern farming practices, though, can change this cycle so that lambs are born earlier, often during the coldest time of the year, to assure that they are ready for slaughter, at four months of age, during the lucrative Easter season. Many never make it to slaughter – they freeze to death soon after birth.

Marcie will never have to lose another baby. She lives at Peaceful Prairie Sanctuary, far from the cruelty of modern animal agriculture.
— *Photos courtesy of Peaceful Prairie Sanctuary*

Cebolla (p. 102) and seven friends were once anonymous faces among more than 600 neglected birds being raised for meat on a farm, many of whom were malnourished and sickly. At Farm Sanctuary's New York Shelter, they have bonded for life, linked not only by their dark pasts, but by their shared desire for comfort, happiness and companionship.
— *Photo by Natalie Bowman*

Arnold (p. 105) lives at United Poultry Concerns but was once being raised for the "delicacy" foie gras — translated literally as "fatty liver." Foie gras ducks are confined in cages or sheds and force-fed several times a day — by thrusting metal pipes down their throats and pushing enormous amounts of grain and fat directly into their gullets — to create a grossly enlarged, fatty liver.
— *Photo by Davida Gypsy Breier*

Burke (p. 103) and his friends were found running loose in Brooklyn. All were about eight weeks old, their age coinciding with an unfortunate annual occurrence: the sale, around Easter, of chicks, ducks and bunnies as "gifts," most of whom are eventually abandoned. Burke and his buddies were rescued and later taken to their permanent home at Farm Sanctuary's New York Shelter.
— *Photo by Natalie Bowman*

Julep (p. 105), a Moulard duckling, was rescued from a foie gras facility where she and many other ducklings were dumped into a trash can, helpless and struggling to survive. Moulards are a breed of duck exploited by the foie gras industry, which considers female hatchlings useless and unfit for production. Now living at Farm Sanctuary's New York Shelter, Julep enjoys the dignity that is her birthright.
— *Photo by Natalie Bowman*

Dot-Dash (p. 103) is a five year old rescued Muscovy-cross duck. Muscovies, who feed by "dabbling," naturally spend the majority of their day in water. Ducks in intensive production facilities, where access to water is limited to nozzle-type drinking devices, never get to swim or forage and are unable to engage in even the most basic of natural behaviors.
— *Photo by Windi Wojdak*

Fiona, Harley, Cornwall (p. 106) and 16 other ducklings were rescued from a man who closed his farm. At Farm Sanctuary, they have a home where their worth is recognized and their needs and desires are met. They swim together, explore in the cool grass together, and fall asleep in their cozy barn each night side by side.
— *Photo by Derek Goodwin*

Sailor (p. 104) was abandoned at a county fairground following a 4-H sale and fair. Geese are fiercely loyal animals and very protective of their families. They mate for life and if a mate is lost they will seclude themselves from other geese and mourn. Happily, Sailor was rescued by Farm Sanctuary and has lived at the organization's California Shelter ever since.
— *Photo by Connie Pugh*

Rescued together from a pet store where the three latched on to one another, **Huey, Duey** and **Sidekick Chick** (p. 106) remained inseparable friends even after coming to Farm Sanctuary. Sadly, Sidekick Chick and Duey have since passed away, but Huey remains at the New York Shelter, where he has thankfully made lots of new friends.
— *Photo by Derek Goodwin*

Delilah, Elijah, Harvey and **Travis** (p. 107) are ducks who were rescued from a horrible cruelty case and given refuge at Farm Sanctuary's California Shelter. They have since been placed in loving, permanent homes through Farm Sanctuary's Farm Animal Adoption Network.
— *Photo by Connie Pugh*

Dutch (p. 108) was found in the back of a rendering truck filled with the byproducts of thousands of dead ducks. He and several other terrified and exhausted ducks were struggling desperately to keep their heads above the blood, manure and other waste in the truck and though they were undoubtedly frightened, they barely resisted their Farm Sanctuary rescuers.
— *Photo by Derek Goodwin*

Down comes from ducks and geese like **Goosifer** (p. 110 at home at Peaceful Prairie.) From the USDA: "When birds are slaughtered, they are first stunned electrically. After their throats are cut (by hand, for geese) and the birds are bled, they are scalded to facilitate removal of large feathers. To remove fine pinfeathers, the birds are dipped in paraffin wax. Down and feathers … are sorted at another facility."
— *Photo by Joanna Lucas*

Aunt Bea, **Barnaby** (p. 114) and **Chrissie** (p. 115) were three of fourteen rabbits found huddled in two cardboard boxes on the shoulder of a New York expressway. The bunnies were terrified by the constant roar of the cars speeding by and were in very real danger of being struck and killed by a passing vehicle. Thankfully, a kind and observant motorist noticed movement in the boxes and stopped to investigate. Shocked by what she found,

the woman gently scooped up the rabbits and placed them in her car. She brought the frightened animals to her small apartment and immediately called Farm Sanctuary for help. Eager to provide safety for the rabbits, they arranged for them to come live at their New York shelter. Two days after they arrived, they were taken to Cornell University's Veterinary Hospital for check-ups and to have them spayed and neutered. The six male rabbits were treated for wounds and the eight females were given a clean bill of health. Barnaby has since been adopted into a loving family; the rest are delighted to have found a home at Farm Sanctuary where they spend their days munching fresh veggies, snuggling in clean straw and enjoying wild romps in their grassy pasture.
— *Photos by Jo-Anne McArthur*

Clover (p. 115), **Warren** (p. 116) and six other rabbits were rescued from a would-be breeder who confined the animals in filthy, bare wire cages in her backyard in New York. The rabbits were kept in crowded cages, exposed to the elements and lying in their own feces and urine. The "owner" of the rabbits did not provide them with regular access to food or water, leaving them dehydrated and hungry. She stated that she had originally purchased the rabbits as "pets" for her kids, but was now breeding them to make money. Eventually, at the urging of a caring neighbor, the breeder agreed to surrender the animals and they were delivered to Farm Sanctuary where they have lived happily ever since.
— *Photos by Jo-Anne McArthur*

Daisy (p. 117) was being sold for food when a kind person whisked her away to safety. Now, she lives a luxurious life with four other rabbits. They enjoy afternoons on their sunny outdoor deck; later, they chase each other and play hide and seek in cardboard boxes positioned especially for them. At night, they enjoy being brushed and massaged by their guardian, Laura. Life is good!
— *Photo by Windi Wojdak*

Farrah and **Damien** (p.118; Farrah, p. 120) live a pampered life now, but they could have been someone's meal. It's hard to know how many rabbits are slaughtered for food in the U.S. The USDA does not provide annual statistics; the most current Rabbit Industry Profile (search www.usda.gov), from 2002, estimates two million. Rabbits do not fall under the Humane Methods of Slaughter Act. Mississippi State University provides the following information on rabbit slaughter: "The preferred method is dislocation of the neck. The rabbit is held firm by the rear legs and head; it is stretched full length. Then with a hard, sharp pull, the head is bent backward to dislocate the neck. The rabbit can also be struck a hard, quick blow to the skull behind the ears. A blunt stick or side of the hand is commonly used …." (www.poultry.msstate.edu/extension/pdf/rabbits_slaughtering.pdf)
— *Photos by Windi Wojdak*

For every egg-laying hen, there is a male like **Lerr** (p. 123) who is killed at the hatchery. Male chicks of egg-laying breeds have no commercial value because they do not grow fast enough or large enough to be economically worthwhile to raise for meat. Instead, one-day-old baby roosters are killed the cheapest way possible, generally by either suffocation or being ground up alive.
— *Photo by Davida Gypsy Breier*

Bumper (p. 124) had been raised as a 4-H livestock project by a young girl who loved and cared for him. When the time came for her to take him to the 4-H judging and auction, she found that the friendship she had with Bumper was so strong that she could not betray his trust. So, with the help of her parents, this compassionate girl found Peaceful Prairie where Bumper is now forever safe and loved.
— *Photo by Davida Gypsy Breier*

Bumper, Laurel, Juliette and **Justice** (p. 125) enjoy each other's company among the rolling hills at Peaceful Prairie Sanctuary, whose website notes: "The animals come in all different sizes and shapes but they all share the same need for a safe loving home and caretakers who respect the lives of each individual animal."
— *Photo by Davida Gypsy Breier*

Abigail and **Daphne** (p. 122) are from a "free-range" facility. It's a popular myth that such places are idyllic. Most are large windowless buildings with a small door. There are no regulations on the amount of outdoor space that must be provided for the hens, or the amount of time they get to spend there. A producer giving 20,000 chickens 20 square feet of outdoor access can label their eggs as "free-range."
— *Photo by Davida Gypsy Breier*

Ernestine (p. 126) was one of 128 pigs left to starve to death or die of exposure on a farm in New York. The pigs were initially taken in by Farm Sanctuary; eventually Ernestine, and nine of her brothers and sisters, came to live at Peaceful Prairie. They now spend their days playing, wallowing, getting into mischief, and enjoying treats.
— *Photo by Davida Gypsy Breier*

Maya (p. 126) was rescued from a family goat dairy and was the last of many males who would have been sold for slaughter as a "byproduct" of dairy production. Fortunately, the family closed their dairy and Maya and the remaining goats now live happily among the Peaceful Prairie herd, where they will stay for the rest of their lives.
— *Photo by Davida Gypsy Breier*

Saffron (p. 130) was a sheep who "came with the house" when the property she lived on went up for sale. Fortunately for her, the new homeowners adored Saffron and were happy to include her as part of their family. She lived the rest of her life cared for and loved until she passed away a few years later.
— *Photo by Windi Wojdak*

Bijou (p. 126) was bred to be a research subject, part of a university's experimental livestock program funded, in part, by citizen tax dollars. He was spared because he was born with bowed back legs, and was rejected from the research project. After weeks of negotiation with the university, Bijou, only two months old, weak, and very under-sized arrived at his safe home, Peaceful Prairie.
— *Photo by Davida Gypsy Breier*

Agnes and **Althea** (p. 131) are Rhode Island Red hens. They, along with sister Kathleen, were rescued from an egg-laying factory farm in Rhode Island. They now spend their days at United Poultry Concerns frolicking in the grass and dust and enjoying watermelon on hot summer days.
— *Photo by Davida Gypsy Breier*

"Sanctuary" was written by Davida Gypsy Breier, during her visit to Peaceful Prairie. On the beautiful, seemingly endless prairie you can see forever, and the sky is huge. The feeling is one of vast openness and freedom. The **goats** (p. 127) running joyfully up the hill embody this feeling perfectly. Would that all beings were allowed to live in this freedom and joy.
— *Photo by Davida Gypsy Breier*

Oliver (p. 132) came to United Poultry Concerns as a young rooster. Later, when 58 hens who were confiscated from a Mississippi cockfighting raid arrived at the sanctuary, he and the hens all moved into a new spacious enclosure built just for them. Oliver is happy and thriving in his new home with his new large family.
— *Photo by Davida Gypsy Breier*

Jean (p. 129) and four other crabs were rescued from a live animal market where he and his tank-mates were destined to be sold and boiled alive. All were released unharmed into the bay where they belong.
— *Photo by Davida Gypsy Breier*

Eva and **Nemo** (p. 133) love to schnuffle in the dirt, but that wasn't always possible for them. Born onto an unheated, cement garage floor, earth wasn't a consideration given them by the misguided couple who wished to raise piglets for slaughter. Rescued and brought to Woodstock Farm Animal Sanctuary, they now spin the schnuffle meter with all the earth they could ever rearrange.
— *Photo by Bob Esposito*

Mackenzie (p. 152) is a resident of United Poultry Concerns. Gentlemanly and dapper with his large red wattles and comb, he was content to stand on the sidelines, watching as the other sanctuary poultry had their photos taken. But when it was his turn, he gallantly struck this striking pose.
— *Photo by Davida Gypsy Breier*

Blitz (p. 153) was once someone's companion animal but was abandoned by his family into a herd of goats who were being raised to be eaten. As a newcomer, he did not fit in well with the established herd. Neighbors noticed his distress and convinced the farmer to let Blitz come live with them. He now has the run of a several acre pasture and has goat friends galore.
— *Photo by Windi Wojdak*

Stanley and **Hardy** (p. 154) were just tiny duck-lings when they were brought to Peaceful Prairie Sanctuary by a wildlife rehabilitation group. Two of the sanctuary's resident geese, Fred and Wilma, immediately adopted the little balls of fluff, and proved to be excellent surrogate parents. Stanley and Hardy grew into healthy, happy adult ducks.
— *Photo by Windi Wojdak*

April (p. 155) and four other hens were adopted from an animal shelter and now live with a family who regularly rescue farmed animals. Just as dogs and cats are abandoned and relinquished to shelters, chickens like April are given up for a variety of reasons ranging from tragic to trivial, heartbreaking to heartless. Adopting any animal from a shelter is a compassionate, life-saving act.
— *Photo by Windi Wojdak*

Clover (p. 157) was being sold at a market when a woman rescued him before he could be made into a meal. Conditions at many of the approximately 200,000 rabbit facilities in the United States are similar to those at a battery-cage egg factory farms. Rabbits are jammed into small cages and most are slaughtered around 10 weeks of age.
— *Photo by Windi Wojdak*

Aubrey (p. 158), the large male turkey at United Poultry Concerns, held great interest for 3-year-old Garnet. He tenderly stroked Aubrey's head and spoke of him for days afterward. Garnet has always been vegan. He thinks cow-burgers, turkey-burgers, or kinkajou-burgers are simply ridiculous. He can't fathom eating an animal — that is his natural state of reason. He inherently understands.
— *Photo by Davida Gypsy Breier*

At just a few days old, **Peep** (p. 160) arrived at a rescue center with his mother. With protective maternal instincts in high-gear, she challenged anyone, bird or human, who came near her beloved only child. This is typical hen behavior — mother hens will threaten other animals who come near their chicks, and will even fight eagles, raccoons and other predators to protect their babies.
— *Photo by Davida Gypsy Breier*

About the Sanctuaries

The Center for Animal Protection and Education (CAPE) is an organization whose goals are to actively educate people about the plight of animals in society today. We provide sanctuary for homeless animals, humane education programs for children and adults, advocacy campaigns addressing current animal issues, and information for people who have specific questions or problems. Through these endeavors, CAPE's aim is to reduce animal suffering, heighten awareness, and bring people and animals together in peaceful co-existence.

CAPE
PO Box 67176,
Scotts Valley, CA 95067-7176
www.capeanimals.org
postmaster@capeanimals.org

Farm Sanctuary is the nation's leading farm animal protection organization. Since incorporating in 1986, Farm Sanctuary has worked to expose and stop cruel practices of the "food animal" industry through research and investigations, legal and institutional reforms, public awareness projects, youth education, and direct rescue and refuge efforts. Farm Sanctuary shelters in Watkins Glen, New York, and Orland, California, provide lifelong care for hundreds of rescued

Mackenzie

animals, who have become ambassadors for farm animals everywhere by educating visitors about the realities of factory farming. Additional information can be found at:

www.farmsanctuary.org
607-583-2225

Peaceful Prairie Sanctuary was founded in 1998 by Michele & Chris Alley-Grubb as an extension of their commitment to vegan advocacy. The Sanctuary has become a Free State for former victims of egg, dairy and flesh production, and our constant inspiration to prioritize vegan advocacy on behalf the billions of captive farmed animals who depend on us to achieve their final emancipation. To that end, Peaceful Prairie Sanctuary does not support or engage in any campaigns that would promote or endorse any animal-derived products labeled as "humane" (i.e. "cage-free," "free-range," "organic," etc.). Go Vegan!

Peaceful Prairie Sanctuary
81053 E. County Road 22
Deer Trail, CO 80105
www.peacefulprairie.org
peacefulprairie@netecin.net
303-769-4997

Poplar Spring Animal Sanctuary is a 400-acre refuge for abused and abandoned farm animals and rehabilitated wildlife. Our mission is to provide a permanent home for rescued farm animals, educate the public about farm animal issues by providing educational tours and presentations, and to promote kindness and compassion for all animals.

Poplar Spring Animal Sanctuary
PO Box 507
Poolesville, MD 20837
www.animalsanctuary.org
info@animalsanctuary.org

United Poultry Concerns is a nonprofit organization dedicated to the compassionate and respectful treatment of chickens, turkeys, ducks and other domestic fowl. We seek to make the public aware of how these birds are treated, and to promote the benefits of a vegan diet and lifestyle. We invite you to join us and support our work. To learn more, contact:

United Poultry Concerns
PO Box 150
Machipongo, VA 23405
www.upc-online.org
Info@upc-online.org
757-678-7875

The **Woodstock Farm Animal Sanctuary** (WFAS) is a non-profit organization that strives to be a voice for farm animals – the most exploited and abused animals in the world. Currently home to over 150 rescued farmed animals at their shelter in the beautiful Catskill Mountains, WFAS works to end the abuse of farmed animals everywhere through farm tours, outreach events, humane education and by promoting a vegan lifestyle. It is a place where visitors can come face to face with "food-production animals" – often for the first time – and learn about the devastating effects of modern-day agribusiness on the animals, the environment and human health. Learn more about Woodstock Farm Animal Sanctuary by visiting their website at:

www.woodstocksanctuary.org
845-679-5955

Blitz

The sanctuaries featured in this book are but a few of dozens across this country, each doing life-saving rescue and educational work. You can find more – including ones in your area – by searching the internet. A good place to start is the sanctuary directory at www.sanctuaries.org (created by Animal Place, www.animalplace.org).

About the Contributors

Michele and **Chris Alley-Grubb** have been vegan for more than 25 years. In 1997, they decided to focus their animal advocacy efforts on the plight of farmed animals. They built Peaceful Prairie Sanctuary and now devote their lives and all of their resources to the sanctuary and its vegan mission.

Natalie Bowman is communications department manager and photographer for Farm Sanctuary. A vegan since the year 2000, she lives with her husband, and 12 incredible rescued cats, dogs and chickens in upstate New York. More of her work can be seen at farmsanctuary.org.

Davida Gypsy Breier started down the path to veganism and animal advocacy as a child after getting to know a family of pigs on a Minnesota farm. She previously worked for The Vegetarian Resource Group and currently works in the publishing industry. As a result of her involvement with No Voice Unheard, she started a new project, Wild Leek Photography, to help support sanctuaries and their residents. Visit www.wildleekphotography.com.

Susie Coston is Farm Sanctuary's national shelter director. Over the past decade, she has mentored many others who have started up their own sanctuaries throughout the US. Currently, she oversees a full staff at the New York Shelter. Aside from working at Farm Sanctuary, Susie cares for her own nine cats, two dogs and two roosters.

Leanne Cronquist, Farm Sanctuary's California shelter director, is a veterinary technician by training. Leanne manages the staff at the California Shelter and ensures the care and well-being of the more than 350 animals who call the west coast sanctuary home. She currently lives at the Shelter itself with her three rescued dogs: Luthien, Beren and Norman.

Stanley & Hardy

Eric Davis has been a veterinarian for 32 years, working with farmed animals, horses, dogs, cats, as well as in academia. A convert to animal protection and rights from a former incarnation as a cowboy, he just wants to help other creatures have better lives and to pay them back for all they have taught him.

Bob Esposito lives and works in New York's Hudson River Valley where the many farm animals and people at Woodstock Farm Animal Sanctuary make it increasingly difficult to consider living and working anywhere else.

Marilee Geyer is a co-founder of No Voice Unheard and lives in northern California with her husband Bob and a variety of rescued animals. She dreams of one day expanding her animal family to include more chickens, some liberated turkeys and goats and maybe even a cow or two (or three or four), or whomever else needs safe sanctuary.

April

Derek Goodwin is a professional photographer and vegan activist in Northampton, Massachusetts. He is the founder of Evolvegan, an organization using creativity to inspire compassion; projects include Vegan Radio, the Vegan Bus, and Veganica.com. His photos of farm animals living at sanctuaries have been published around the world in books, magazines and on the web.

Erin Howard, a vegan since 2004, is the photo and video coordinator at Farm Sanctuary's headquarters in upstate New York. She credits her passion for photography to the incredible lives and personalities of farm animals, whose stories often go untold.

Diane Leigh is co-author of *One at a Time: A Week in an American Animal Shelter* and co-founder of No Voice Unheard. She dreams – with love, hope, and action – of a luminous, shining world in which all beings are respected and left to live in peace.

Joanna Lucas is a writer, artist, and designer whose work strives to explore, document and present the inner lives of the most systematically abused, most willfully excluded group of individuals on earth: farmed animals. She is honored to work with Peaceful Prairie Sanctuary and to know and tell the stories of the farmed animal refugees themselves.

Lesley Marino is a Toronto-based photographer who uses her camera to tell the stories of her subjects, both human and animal. An animal rights advocate and vegetarian for over 20 years, she is excited to be part of a project that gives voices to those who cannot speak for themselves.

Jo-Anne McArthur has been working as a photojournalist since 1998 and has traveled to over 40 countries with her camera. Sometimes she thinks her camera is just an excuse for meeting people and documenting their stories. These days, most of Jo-Anne's energy is spent abroad, documenting the abuses that animals suffer at the hands of humans for an upcoming book called *We Animals*. Visit: www.weanimals.org and www.joannemcarthur.com.

Connie Pugh is a registered nurse by profession and a farmed animal photographer by passion. She hopes to teach the world the beauty and relevance of farm animals through photography. She spends her off-work hours volunteering at Farm Sanctuary in Orland, California, where she has hundreds of dear animal friends.

Jean Rhode splits her time between Brooklyn and Woodstock, where the cows, pigs, chickens, goats, tukeys sheep and ducks at Woodstock Farm Animal Sanctuary continue to change her life. You can read more about these animals who are often ignored but are so amazing, loving and wonderful on Jean's blog: www.jeanrhode.com/animals/Blog/Blog.html.

Kit Salisbury has been an ethical vegetarian since she was 18 years old and has been involved in animal rights/welfare issues for the past 35 years. Kit is currently the department manager of the Cogut Center for the Humanities at Brown University in Providence, Rhode Island.

Windi Wojdak has dedicated most of her life's work to animal protection and advocacy and is continually in awe of the resiliency of spirit of those who suffer and those who strive to relieve suffering. She believes in bearing witness and in the power to create change by living each moment in alignment with our deepest principles.

Clover

To Learn More

Although the world is full of suffering, it is full also of the overcoming of it. — Helen Keller

There are many excellent books, web sites, organizations and other resources available to help you find additional information on farmed animals, factory farming and adopting a vegetarian or vegan diet. There are so many, in fact, that it would be impossible to list them all, so what follows are some of our favorites. Each will lead to many more where you'll find information, encouragement, and inspiration...

Diet for a New America: How Your Food Choices Affect Your Health, Happiness and the Future of Life on Earth, by John Robbins (Stillpoint Publishing, 1987.) For many of us, this book was the first we'd ever read on the topic of vegetarianism and factory farming — and it changed our lives forever. It is widely considered to be one of the most influential books on health, compassion, and the environment ever written.

Farm Sanctuary: Changing Hearts and Minds About Animals and Food, by Gene Baur, (Touchstone, 2008.) Written by Farm Sanctuary's President, this book is an insightful look at the ethical questions involved in the use of animals for food. He explains how all of us can make a better life for ourselves and animals.

Aubrey & Garnet

Prisoned Chickens, Poisoned Eggs: An Inside Look at the Modern Poultry Industry, by Karen Davis (revised edition, Book Publishing Co., 2009.) This book looks at a world in which avian flu, food poisoning, global warming, genetic engineering, and expanding poultry production are careening to an unsustainable point, and provides a compelling case for adopting compassionate, plant-based cuisine.

Quantum Wellness: A Practical Guide to Health and Happiness, by Kathy Freston (Weinstein Books, 2009.) The best-selling author who inspired Oprah to go vegan for a month presents an approach to increasing the health of mind, body and spirit using small steps that yield big changes. She provides an eating plan that minimizes harm to oneself and other creatures.

The Face On Your Plate: The Truth About Food, by Jeffrey Moussaieff Masson (W.W. Norton & Company, 2009.) The best-selling author of *When Elephants Weep* delves into the psychological factors that influence decisions about what we eat and why — and how those choices affect our lives, animals' lives, and the environment.

The Food Revolution: How Your Diet Can Help Save Your Life and Our World, by John Robbins (Conari Press, 2001.) This book will tell you the truth about popular diets, genetically modified foods, mad cow disease and the health effects of what you eat. It shows you how to extend your life, increase your vitality, and take a stand for a more compassionate and sustainable world.

The Pig Who Sang to the Moon: The Emotional World of Farm Animals, by Jeffrey Moussaieff Masson (Ballantine Books, 2004.) Weaves together history, literature, anecdotes and scientific discoveries to beautifully present the complex emotional lives of farmed animals. You may never be able to look at farmed animals in the same way again.

VegNews is the premier magazine focusing on a vegetarian lifestyle, offering information on living a compassionate and healthy lifestyle with the latest vegetarian news, interviews, travel tales, features on food and health, recipes, the hottest new veg products, vegan weddings, and celebrity buzz. www.vegnews.com

Compassionate Cooks is a resource for recipes, book reviews and information about vegetarianism that gives people the tools they need to optimize their health and live in a manner benefiting the Earth and its inhabitants. www.compassionatecooks.com

Compassion Over Killing offers a free, 24-page "Vegetarian Starter Guide," by mail or download. The booklet contains information on nutrition, shopping, and helpful tips. www.tryveg.com/request

Happy Cow is a searchable directory of vegetarian and vegan restaurants and natural health food stores. The site includes thousands of listings and reviews, as well as a community forum. www.happycow.net

Vegan Outreach is a nonprofit organization dedicated to reducing the suffering of farmed animals by promoting informed, ethical eating. www.veganoutreach.org

The Vegetarian Resource Group is a nonprofit organization whose mission is to educate the public on vegetarianism and the interrelated issues of health, nutrition, ecology, ethics and world hunger. www.vrg.org

VegPeople is a vegan and vegetarian "online community" offering discussion boards on animals, food and fitness, recipes, philosophy and more. www.vegpeople.com

VegWeb is a recipe "swap" site where you can browse an extensive collection of user-created and reviewed vegan recipes. www.vegweb.com

Veg for Life, a Farm Sanctuary website, is a comprehensive information and networking site filled with hundreds of resources, recipes and tips to help you on your veg journey. www.vegforlife.com

Vegan at Heart is a free e-mail coaching program for people who are vegan at heart but not necessarily in practice. As a subscriber, you will receive one vegan "mission" every day for 30 days. Each mission takes just minutes to complete. www.kindgreenplanet.org/programs/veganatheart/welcome

Peep

Thank You

No Voice Unheard thanks these generous supporters who made this book possible…

Lynne Achterberg and Margret Rinner/Project Purr, Deborah Beards, Mary Beth Brown,
Tom Campbell and the Guacamole Fund, Dave Canino and Paula Ash,
The Center for Animal Protection and Education, Nell Cliff and the Porter Sesnon Foundation,
Stephen Colley, James Corcoran, Sandee Davis, Janet Davis, Katarina and Tom Donohue,
Mark Damian Fowler, Barbara Goodrich, Carmel Granger, Diane Hamelin, Wendy Hyatt,
Virginia Kallianes, Monique Leduc, Barbara Lee, Meryl Lewin, Robyn Nayyar, Coleen O'Brien,
Elena Owens, Sylvia Pascal, Mary Rigdon, Kit Salisbury, Patsy Volpe, Wild Leek Photography

**And our heartfelt thanks to those who kindly shared
with us their time, talent, and wisdom…**

Michele and Chris Alley-Grubb, Heather Bechtel/The Rabbit Haven, Walter Bond, Jenny Brown,
Susie Coston, Leanne Cronquist, Terry Cummings, Eric & Ila Davis, Karen Davis, Bob Esposito, Derek
Goodwin, Nanette Hardin and David Zollo, Erin Howard, Gail Pope & Fray Huffman/BrightHaven,
Chad Johnson, Key West Wildlife Rescue, Laura Lawn, Joanna Lucas, Lesley Marino,
Jo-Anne McArthur, JP Novic, Karen Oeh & Mike Balistreri, Amber Plaut,
Connie Pugh, Jean Rhode, Todd Stosuy, Jessica Strader

Gratitude to Davida Gypsy Breier, Natalie Bowman, Mike Miller and Kit Salisbury for
their dedication to and help with this project. Without them, this book would not exist.

And our deepest personal thanks to…

Bob Geyer and Gilly, Minnie and Willy;
Patrick, Garnet, Janette and Earl;
Andrea Lee; Kathy Ninneman; Kevin

ALL OUR RELATIONS

More Titles from No Voice Unheard

One at a Time
A Week in an American Animal Shelter

With compelling photographs and moving vignettes, chronicles the true stories of 75 dogs and cats who passed through a typical U.S. shelter during seven days witnessed and documented by the authors, Diane Leigh and Marilee Geyer.

Winner of the Humane Society of the United States Pets for Life Award, the ASPCA Humane Issues Award, and a Cat Writers Muse Medallion.

"A must read – it will change your life."
– Mark Bekoff, author of *Wild Justice: the Moral Lives of Animals*

160 pages, 9″ x 10″, 75 duotone photos, softcover, ISBN 0972838708

Thought to Exist in the Wild
Awakening from the Nightmare of Zoos

Combining stunning photographs and a riveting essay, offers an unflinching philosophical consideration of our relations with animals and wild nature, and asks how zoos teach us to perceive nonhuman animals and our relationship to them. Written by award-winning author Derrick Jensen, with photographs by Karen Tweedy-Holmes.

Winner of the Grand Prize in the Eric Hoffer Book Awards.

"Finally someone has the courage to question zoos. This is a brave book and a much needed voice on behalf of the animals." – Bill Maher, host of HBO's *Real Time with Bill Maher*

152 pages, 10″ x 9″, 83 duotone photos, softcover (limited edition hardcover available only from the publisher), ISBN 9780972838719

No Voice Unheard is a non-profit publisher whose goal is to educate and inform. We strive to make our titles as accessible as possible, and offer substantial discounts to other non-profit organizations.

We also offer a Giving Package program to individuals – a special discount on packages of 5 books, to give as gifts or donations to schools, libraries, coffee houses, community centers or any place where the books can reach the public. Other recipients might include teachers, clergy, legislators and policy makers, community leaders, celebrities, activists in other fields and anyone who can affect social change.

Please contact us or visit our website for more information.

NO VOICE UNHEARD
PO Box 4171 • Santa Cruz, CA 95063 • (831) 440-9574
info@novoiceunheard.org • www.NoVoiceUnheard.org

Donations to No Voice Unheard are tax deductible. Your contribution will help underwrite the expenses associated with producing our books, so that proceeds from their sales can be used for educational outreach.

No Voice Unheard titles are distributed to the trade by: National Book Network
4501 Forbes Blvd., Suite 200 • Lanham , MD 20706
Phone (800) 462-6420 • Fax (800) 338-4550